Musical Performance,
1997, Vol. 1, Part 2
Reprints available directly from the publisher
Photocopying permitted by license only

CW01072431

THE PERFORMANCE OF JEWISH AND ARAB MUSIC IN ISRAEL TODAY
Edited by Amnon Shiloah
In two parts

Contents: Part 1

A CD with examples of Arab Music, played by the Arab Music Orchestra in Israel, Yiddish song, Klezmer, and Judeo-Spanish song will be issued with Part 2 of *The Performance of Jewish and Arab Music in Israel Today.*

Musical Performance,
1997, Vol. 1, Part 2, pp. 1–3
Reprints available directly from the publisher
Photocopying permitted by license only

Introduction

Amnon Shiloah

Israel, with its highly heterogeneous immigrant society, offers to the observer a fascinating instance of multifaceted performance practice. Within a relatively limited area there are numerous musical traditions and styles which encompass sacred and secular, old and new, folk and sophisticated forms.

The ten contributions included in the two issues dealing with the performance of Jewish and Arab music in Israel today represent an attempt to cover the most significant traditions that were established during the period before 1948: the search for the establishment of a new and typically Israeli art and folk music; the attitude of the protagonists of this tendency toward the old exiled traditional heritage of the Jewish people, and the struggle of the immigrants after the creation of the State of Israel to ensure the survival of their musical traditions as well as to cope with the new physical and cultural environment. Altogether the general scope of these contributions correspond to a large extent to major events which have marked the musical and cultural history of modern Israel from the 1920s to the 1990s, including local Arab music which is also dealt with in the contributions. Thus, it is not surprising to find that a key phenomenon, predominant in most of the articles, is change. Indeed, there is no single tradition that has not been transformed in some way.

The mass transfer of the different ethnic traditions that followed the establishment of the State of Israel in 1948 found Israeli society at the height of a long struggle over the nature of the new culture that would and should appropriately reflect the rebirth of the Jewish nation in its ancient land. Under the pressure of circumstances, the central aspiration – to create one unified people from many heterogeneous elements – gained momentum. In searching for an appropriate identity, music played an important role. In the attempts to create a national style in music from the 1920s onwards one finds many and varied tendencies that range from a call for total adherence to the great musical achievements of the West, with an emphasis on the universal aspects of the new national aspirations, to the urge to adopt the Orient as a source of inspiration.

This struggle between antagonistic tendencies in the quest for a national identity in music and other aspects of the culture, is the background of the first contribution in this issue. In his study *Performers between East and West – Ideology and Reality in the Yishuv*, the musicologist and historian of music in Modern Israel, Jehoash Hirshberg, provides a theoretical overview, which reflects the conflicting views; the ideological pressure emanating from the desire to use the vision of the East as a source for inspiration, as against the prevailing total adherence to the models of the West. In his historical survey Hirshberg touches upon major questions and aspects on which other contributors shed further light. This is the case with Natan Shahar's study which concentrates on his area of specialization:

Israeli folk song in its communal performance manifestation, focusing on its latest form, the establishment of the so-called performing "song companies". The author's point of departure is the premise that the novel ways followed by those performing groups derive directly from the former practice of spontaneous communal singing in the collective settlements (the Kibbutzim) where it fulfilled a highly social and cultural role. This study refers to recent research carried out by the author.

There is no doubt that in the quest for a national style, protagonists and supporters of the vision of the East drew inspiration from local Arab folk and art music with which they were in constant contact. The most authentic and pervasive kind of Arab music has been the rich folk music which enhanced the events in the life of Bedouins, farmers and, to certain extent, town dwellers. Yet, the latter also enjoyed the pleasure of sophisticated art music. However, one should note that local art music has been essentially dependant on the Lebanese, Syrian, and Egyptian classical and "mainstream" or modernized styles. In his contribution, Suheil Radwan a Christian-Arab musician who for more than four decades has been involved in many musical manifestations and educational activities, provides an eyewitness survey of the development of Arab music in Israel. In many of the activities described by the author, Muslim, Christian and Jewish musicians worked side by side. The Jewish musicians who came from such Arab countries as Iraq, Egypt and Syria, were already distinguished musicians in their own countries. One of them, the outstanding 'ūd player and composer, Ezra Aharon, who represented his former country Iraq at the first International Congress of Arabic music held in 1932 in Cairo, was the founder in 1957 of the official professional Oriental ensemble of the Israeli Radio. Interestingly, this ensemble which included local Arab musicians, and performed for mixed audiences, did not admit excellent musicians from North Africa, Iran and Central Asia, perhaps due to stylistic incompatibility.

The other contributions in this issue, deal with religious musical traditions in their present forms; that is to say, after more than four decades of exposure to Israeli culture, and particularly after the effort of the establishment to apply its 'melting pot' ideology of creating Israelis out of the new immigrants, that would have had them abandon their original cultures. One can see, however, that despite circumstances, traditional music still continues to be vital, especially in religious practices, and to a certain extent in family and community events.

Nevertheless, transformations occurred, even in the highly functional music of the synagogue whose first aim has been to enhance prayer, avoiding as much as possible conscious artistry. Thus, one can witness not only the invasion of elements borrowed from Israeli folk music into sacred music, but also the growing adoption of aesthetic ideals and concepts based on the norms of both Western and Near Eastern art music and their performance practices. Instances of increasing professional demands on cantors, the formalization of their training, concert-like performances of cantorial music, and the place given to them in the media and the like, are among the changes that both Raymond Goldstein and Ezra Barnea point out in their respective articles on Ashkenazi and Sephardi cantorial music.

In part 2 of *The Performance of Jewish and Arab Music in Israel Today* the two prestigious repertoires from the past – Yiddish and Judeo-Spanish Songs – are investigated in articles by Gila Flam and Susanna Weich-Shahak. Avi Bar-Eitan writes about the thriving Klezmer tradition in Israel and Galit Einav Nissinbaum describes the music that accompanies Belly Dancing, which has become a social event. Amy Horowitz, who contributes the final article, *Performance of Disputed Territories: Israeli Mediterranean Music*, deals with an interesting trend, a new style of music that combines traditional Jewish elements with popular Greek and Arab music.

Musical Performance,
1997, Vol. 1, Part 2, pp. 5–13
Reprints available directly from the publisher
Photocopying permitted by license only

Performers between East and West – Ideology and Reality in the *Yishuv*

Jehoash Hirshberg

The history of performance in the Jewish community of Palestine before the foundation of Israel provides a rare opportunity for the study of the emergence of musical life in a highly heterogeneous immigrant society from its inception. Music served both as a powerful tool for social unification of the heterogeneous immigrant community and as means for preserving past ethnic ties. Eastern ethnic groups preserved their in-context performance, whereas the immigrants from Europe transplanted institutional models as means for social interaction. Based on the model of dichotomy of compartmentalization vs. syncretism, the study shows that despite ideologically motivated attempts at merging east and west, compartmentalization won the upper hand.

KEY WORDS   *Yishuv*, East West, Compartmentalization, Syncretism, Active audience.

A historian of performance practice in a given country would most likely commence his search not only by tracing the point in time when it all began but also by an attempt to explain the circumstances, whether economic, sociological, or ideological, which determined the subsequent direction selected by the performing groups under discussion.[1] Yet, while it is frequently possible to determine the precise date of the founding of a particular orchestra or opera company, it is much more difficult to determine the extent to which they resemble or differ from similar preceding ventures. The history of performance in the *Yishuv*[2] provides a rare opportunity to study the emergence of musical life in a highly heterogeneous immigrant society from its inception. In this article I want to turn from the detailed historical discussion I have employed in a recent historical study of musical life in the *Yishuv*[3] to a theoretical overview of the long range developments which determined not only what happened but also what prevented the realization of certain implications in a society where the absence of any precedent rendered any direction at least theoretically possible.

Historical Background

The *Yishuv* was a heterogeneous immigrant society which evolved by fits and starts, with sudden large waves of immigration followed by brief periods of depression and emigration. A small Jewish community of religiously committed orthodox Jews slowly emerged in Palestine, then under Ottoman rule, after 1840.

[1]   See Cyril Ehrlich, *The Music Profession in Britain since the Eighteenth Century* (Oxford, 1985, 1988).

[2]   Literally, 'settlement', denotes the autonomous Jewish community in Palestine from 1840 to the establishment of the State of Israel in 1948.

[3]   *Music in the Jewish Community of Palestine 1880–1948 A Social History* (Oxford, 1995).

In 1839 there were only 8000 Jews in Palestine, most of them of the *Sephardi* community. By 1914 their numbers had increased by tenfold to 80,000, and the number of *Ashkenazi* Jews slightly exceeded that of the *Sephardi*.[4] The year 1882 marked the beginning of nationally motivated Jewish immigration from Eastern Europe, at the same time as the arrival of religiously committed Jews from Yemen. The hardships of World War I depleted the small community and halted nearly all cultural activities, but the establishment of British rule over Palestine in 1918 encouraged an intensive renewal of Jewish immigration, first from Russia and Poland, and after 1930 also from central Europe. Between 1918 and the onset of World War II in 1939 the *Yishuv* grew ninefold from 50,000 to 445,000. It was a highly heterogeneous society. Jews and Arabs lived together in the mixed cities Jerusalem and Haifa and in adjacent towns such as Jaffa and Tel Aviv, to which was added the pronounced presence of Europeans, whether as part of the British administration or as religious Christian communities, such as the German colonies in Jerusalem and in Jaffa.

Jewish immigration was motivated by a constantly varying combinations of push-pull powers.[5] Persecutions and discrimination in the countries of origin coupled with a religious and national commitment to the revival of Jewish life in the ancient homeland drew some of the Jewish immigration from Europe into Palestine. The Jews in Palestine were split into numerous ethnic groups, some observing and conservative, others socialist and secular. The languages and customs of their countries of origin were carried over into Palestine. The national ideology of the European Jews countered the forces of separation by a powerful social action which strove to unify the *Yishuv* through the deliberate implementation of the daily use of modernized Hebrew and the encouragement of social activities as the spearhead of unification. Public musical events, such as active group singing in Hebrew and social gatherings in concerts were favoured by the political and cultural leadership of the *Yishuv*.

The Vision of the East

Foremost in the national ideology was the Vision of the East which signified the rejection of the past life of the Jews in Europe and progress towards the establishment of a proud new way of life. The romanticized image of the biblical farmer turned agricultural and physical labour into the epitome of the national movement. The Arab farmer or Bedouin was idealized as preserving the biblical way of life, and the modern kibbutz[6] was revered also by those who chose urban

---

[4]   Yehoshua Ben Arieh, 'The *Yishuv* in *Eretz Israel* on the Eve of Zionist Settlement', in *The Otto-man Period*, 75. Jerusalem, 1989.

[5]   Egon F. Kunz, 'The Refugee in Flight: Kinetic Models and Forms of Displacement.' *International Migration Review* 7 (1973), 125–46. Ruben G. Rumbaut, Portraits, Patterns, and Predictors of the Refugee Adaptation Process: Results and Reflections from the IHARP Panel Study.' *Refugees as immigrants Cambodians, Laotians and Vietnamese in America*, David W. Hains ed. Totowa, N. J 1989.

[6]   A collective agricultural settlement in which all members contribute by hard work to the benefit of the collective and all financial resources and property are equally shared. The kibbutz movement gathered momentum after World War I, and from 1921 to 1948 the number of *kibbutzim* in Palestine leaped from 11 to 130 and their population increased from about 700 in 1921 to 54,000.

dwelling. Young Jewish dancers eschewed their classical ballet shoes and danced bare-foot, wearing Arab dress as representations of biblical figures. Such circumstances turned the phenomenon of public performance into an ideological declaration. Yet, the ideology alone could not erase the deeply ingrained western heritage from the consciousness of the European Jews. The east-west encounter may best be illustrated by a pair of conflicting statements by music loving literary figures. One year after his immigration in 1911 the young poet Ya'akov Koplewitz (1892–1977), wrote in his memoirs: 'The one thing which I missed more than everything in Jerusalem was music. I was a music lover since my youth . . . The Italian opera tunes which my old Polish friend, Pan Kahl, had played to me in my home town, and the pleasing Russian Waltzes which the cavalry band used to play at dawn while riding for drills through the sleeping town, had awakened in me the desire for the art of music with its penetrating magic. I found nothing of all that in Jerusalem . . . The Arabic ornamental singing which used to come out of old gramophones here and there in the Old City or at the Arab cafe near Jaffa Gate, and the eastern chanting of our brethren the Jews of Babylon and Syria, accompanied by their monotonous harp, did not sound to my ears as music at all, but as part of the exotic outlines of the environment. I could not hear them for more than a quarter of an hour without succumbing to an oppressive feeling of alienation'.[7] By contrast, the poet and columnist Yehudah Karni (1884–1949) requested that the immigrant artist undergo a deep transformation: 'You must keep quiet for a while, and in your silence try to free yourself of all impressions and sounds in which you had been engulfed in the diaspora. . . . The wild cry which one hears in this country at an Arab wedding is more significant for the Hebrew art of the future than the formal European tune, and the dances of our road construction workers are more important than the most modern foreign dances. We must learn from the Sephardim and from the Yemenites.'[8] An extremely small group of musicians and amateurs led by the physician Mordecai Sandberg (1898–1973) advocated a total segregation of the *Yishuv* from the West in order to absorb the influence of the East. Sandberg had a quarter-tone harmonium built to his order by Straube in Germany.[9] Yet, his views were ridiculed by the active professional musicians and little noticed by the audience at large so that a total rejection of the West and the establishment of an absolutely Oriental musical culture in the *Yishuv* was never seriously considered.

Performance in Context

In their classification of stylistic dynamics, Shiloah and Cohen have made a distinction between the internal audience, that is, members of the musician's own

[7]   Yeshurun Keshet, (Ya'akov Koplewitz's later Hebraized name), *Kedma Veyama (East and West)*, 34. Tel Aviv, 1980.

[8]   *Hedim* 1 (1922), 37–8 (A literary Hebrew periodical).

[9]   On the brink of World War II Sandberg was cut off from Palestine while lecturing in New York. In 1970 he moved to Toronto. His two micro-tone instruments have been temporarily placed at the Department of Music, York University, Toronto. They are in need of a thorough repair.

ethnic community, and an external audience.[10] Generally speaking, the two types correspond to the difference in the social structure of the eastern *Sephardi* Jewish groups and the immigrants from Europe most of whom were *Ashkenazi* Jews. The former as a rule lived in expanded families and within their own ethnic community, around their synagogue. The latter consisted mostly of relatively young unmarried individuals and young couples who were separated from their expanded families. Consequently, while the oriental Jews could satisfy all their social and emotional needs within their homes and immediate environment, the Europeans felt the urge to mix with other people. The mild Mediterranean climate, the absence of any home entertainment (at least until 1936 when very limited radio broadcasting started), and the cramped living conditions further encouraged social gatherings.

The traditional pattern which dominated the Oriental Jewish ethnic groups consisted of performances of music in liturgical, paraliturgical, and family and community events for an internal audience. Distinction between active performers and passive listeners was often blurred, with the congregation frequently joining in, singing and playing.[11] By contrast, the European pattern consisted of public concerts, performed on stage in auditoriums for ethnically diverse concert goers not necessarily familiar with each others. The national ideology pressured composers and performers raised on the European model to turn to the East, an act which would have required immigrant musicians struggling for their daily bread and lacking training or predilection to anthropological fieldwork, to find their way into the enclosed eastern communities.

The following adaptation of existing models of change will chart the outcome of the ideologically-motivated encounter of the two conflicting patterns in the field of performance.[12] For the present purposes the graded typology which characterizes the models will be replaced by a system of three polarized opposites stemming from the dichotomy of **COMPARTMENTALIZATION – SYNCRETISM**

1. INTERNAL AUDIENCE – EXTERNAL AUDIENCE

2. ACTIVE CONGREGATION – PASSIVE LISTENERS

3. WESTERN AND ORIENTAL INSTRUMENTS SEPARATED – MIXED

1. Compartmentalization. Originally defined as a subcategory of pluralistic coexistence of musics,[13] this category signifies the co-existence in Palestine of transplanted European ensembles and traditional eastern in-context performance.

---

[10]   Amnon Shiloah & Eric Cohen, 'The Dynamics of Change in Jewish Oriental Ethnic Music in Israel', *Ethnomusicology*, 27 (1983), 237.

[11]   For a detailed discussion, see Amnon Shiloah, *Jewish Musical Traditions* (Detroit, 1992), 162–180. The ethnic division prevailed especially in Jerusalem and is obvious to the present day. See Yehoshua Ben-Arieh, *A City Reflected in its Times – the Old City* (Jerusalem 1977); *Jerusalem in the 19th Century*, (New York, 1986).

[12]   Margaret Kartomi, 'The Processes and Results of Musical Culture Contact: A Discussion of Terminology and Concepts.' *Ethnomusicology* 25 (1981) 227–249. Bruno Nettl, 'Some Aspects of the Theory of World Music in the Twentieth Century: Questions, Problems, and Concepts.' *Ethnomusicology* 22 (1978), 123–36.

[13]   Margaret Kartomi, 'The Processes and Results of Musical Culture Contact: A Discussion of Terminology and Concepts.' '*Ethnomusicology* 25 (1981), 237.

The process of compartmentalization was a direct outcome of an attempt, by immigrants from Europe, to soften the objective trauma of re-settlement through the subjective factor of transplanted cultural life.[14] The entire infra-structure of public musical life of the *Yishuv* had been established by 1936, despite extreme changes and reversals in the economic and social conditions which caused the quick collapse of some of the ventures, most importantly the pioneering Palestine Opera under Mark Golinkin (1923–7), whereas others, such as the Palestine Orchestra (since 1949 the Israel Philharmonic Orchestra)[15] persevered to the present day. The urge to transplant the European performing ensembles was so powerful, that Golinkin initiated his operative venture with a mere 23 members, an unpaid pupils' orchestra; this gradually turned into an underpaid 40 piece professional ensemble. Sarah Golinkin, the conductor's daughter, regularly filled in the missing parts (mostly for the harp) on the piano.[16]

Compartmentalization retained in most cases the traditional distinction between external audience for the public concert and internal one for the traditional, eastern performances. Yet, the social composition of Jerusalem and Tel Aviv, though utterly different from one another, led to the adaptation of the pattern of internal audience to that of the public concert through the flowering of numerous concert societies.

The population of cosmopolitan Jerusalem was fragmented into numerous small ethnic, religious, and cultural communities. The Jerusalem Music Society was the product of the cultural Jerusalem elite.

Led by the cellist Thelma Yellin, the Society ran more than fifteen seasons of classic-romantic chamber concerts, most of them given by the Jerusalem String Quartet, at times in private homes and usually in small, intimate auditoriums.

The membership consisted of British officials, well-to-do Arabs, the ancient Sephardi families, most of the then small faculty of the Hebrew University (founded 1925), and the Zionist leadership. Though ethnically and religiously heterogeneous, the membership comprised the social and intellectual elite of Jerusalem and most of them had known each other from personal and business daily encounter. The membership assured a regularly balanced budget and the Society even granted fellowships to needy music students.

The majority of the Tel Aviv audience frequently displayed unruly behaviour at concerts of all kinds, such as noisy entering of late-comers, applauding at the wrong spots, culminating with one case when a patron brought his dog along to a concert. Deeply hurt by that which for them amounted to sacrilege, a group of sophisticated music lovers from Tel Aviv established a small elite Music Society whose concerts were open by membership only.

After one of the Music Society concerts in Tel Aviv a member of the Society is quoted by the critic David Rosolio as saying: This is the first time since my immigration that I sense the typical mood which prevails at the European

---

[14] John Goldust & A.H. Richmond, 'Multivariate Model of Immigrant Adaptation', International Migration Review, 8 (1974), 193–223.

[15] Jehoash Hirshberg, 'Israel Philharmonic Orchestra', Robert Craven, ed., *Symphony Orchestras of the World* (New York, London, 1987), 202–9.

[16] Interview, March 1991. Such economizing was not exceptional in the 1920s, cf. Cyril Ehrlich, *The Music Profession in England* (Oxford, 1985), 208.

auditoriums'.[17] The elite societies turned the performance of chamber music into a ritual for an internal audience, a characteristic that, in part, has persisted to the present day.[18]

Thus, the establishment of the societies, albeit of similar nature, led to contrasting social results. The chamber music societies unified otherwise hetero-geneous population groups in Jerusalem, whereas they caused a split within the otherwise homogeneous population of Tel Aviv.

2. The Audience as an Active Participant. There have been many cases in which performers have tried to overcome the blunt separation between active performers on stage and a passive audience in the auditorium. Most prevalent in western musical life has been the tradition of audience participation in some movements of large scale choral pieces, such as final chorales in church cantatas, as well as at popular performances of Handel's *Messiah* when the audiences (in England and the USA) join in the choral movements.

The national ideology of the *Yishuv* was especially conducive to the blurring of the dividing line between performer and listener. Occasionally it occurred spontaneously, as, for example, when violinist Samuel Dushkin played a series of folk song arrangements for violin and piano and the audience joined in humming the well-known tunes.[19] There were, however, two institutionalized venues for the audience as an active performer.

In the towns the audience gathered for communal singing of folk song. Lacking a common heritage of Hebrew folk song, the *Yishuv* encouraged the composition and dissemination of new Hebrew songs which covered the entire range of the *Yishuv's* life, from eulogizing the scenery of Palestine to socialist work songs and national marches. Central authorities such as the Cultural Centre of the Federation of Hebrew Workers sponsored regular gatherings of 'public singing'. Held in auditoriums, they were planned and guided by a professional coach who distributed mimeographed copies of the texts, accompanied the singing on the accordion or another instrument, and instructed the audience in one or two brand new songs each evening. The ticket price was minimal and the place was always sold out.

The rural venue was the celebration of the traditional Jewish holidays in the kibbutz movement. The collective and secular kibbutz ideology contradicted both the religious service and the family meals which are the core of each traditional Jewish holiday. The kibbutz re-interpreted the Jewish holidays as modern revivals of ancient biblical agricultural rites. Of special importance was the Passover *Seder* which was held in the kibbutz dining hall, with all the members and their children present, together with guests and family members from town. Each kibbutz had its own version, which went through yearly modifications according to the available local performers. A balance was always kept between sections which were performed by the *kibbutz* choruses, solo singers, and instrumentalists, and those in which the entire congregation joined. Certain versions of the *Seder*, most notably that of kibbutz *Yagur* which were edited, partly composed, and coached by composer Yehudah Sharet, became a model for other *kibbutzim*.

---

[17]   David Rosolio, 'The music Society and its Activities', *Ha'Aretz* 4 Dec 1927.

[18]   Philip V. Bohlman, *The Land where Two Streams Flow* (Illinois, 1989).

[19]   *Davar* 12 April 1927.

3. East–West Syncretism.   Attempts to combine Oriental and European instruments went through two stages. The easier and more frequent was the ideologically motivated transfer of eastern ethnic music to the context of the public concert. The earliest event on record was a modest ceremony which took place in Jerusalem in December 1885 when the poverty-stricken Yemenite Jews entered the first houses built for them in Silwan village. The two Hebrew newspapers reported that there were many guests on that occasion, who were very excited to hear the Yemenite traditional songs.[20] A breakthrough came in the 1930s with the public concerts of Yemenite singers Bracha Zefira, Sara Osnat Halevi, and later Esther Gamlielit. The most influential was Zefira (1910–1990) who first toured the country with improvising Russian-born pianist Nahum Nardi, thus combining her repertory of Jewish eastern traditional tunes with the most European of instruments. In 1939 she turned to pre-composed arrangements by professional immigrant composers from Europe which she performed with chamber ensembles of members of the Palestine Orchestra.[21] Her many recordings indicate that the differences in intonation were either ignored or smoothed down. Yet, Zefira was hardly pleased with the sound production of western instruments, especially of strings. In her autobiography she wrote that once she asked the players to play without vibrato, to arpeggiate chords, and to strike the wooden backs of the instruments with their fingers. All her requests were rejected and she finished the rehearsal 'depressed and pessimistic'.[22] Another unsuccessful attempt at modifying a western instrument was made by composer and pianist Alexander U. Boskovitch. In 1941 the dancer Yardena Cohen started to employ three Jewish fishmongers of Iraqi origin to accompany her allegedly biblical dances on the *darabukka*, the *'ūd*, and the Arabic flute. After two years of abrasive relationships with them she turned to Boskovitch in 1944 and asked him to arrange the dances for the piano. While at work at her studio, Boskovitch tried to insert thin napkins between the hammers and the strings in order to modify the sound of the piano, but he soon gave up this awkward attempt.[23] The original orchestral version of Boskovitch's *Semitic Suite* included a part for cymbalom as an imitation of the *qānūn*, betraying the influence of Kodaly's *Hary Janos*, but the instrument was not available and the part was deleted at the premiere and never restored.

A more daring attempt at combining genuine Arabic and European instruments was taken by the *'ūd* player and composer Ezra Aharon, a fine professional musician who immigrated from Iraq in 1935. In 1936 the Palestine Broadcast Service was founded, transmitting on a single channel and alternating daily between English, Arabic, and Hebrew programmes. Aharon was hired to run the Hebrew programme, a daily broadcast of Arabic and eastern-Jewish music with a small ensemble, alongside the Studio Players which was the nucleus of the forthcoming radio orchestra. The programme director Karl Salomon encouraged

---

[20]   *Havatzelet*, 10, *Hazevi*, 9, 1885. Silwan is an Arab village on the steep slope opposite the Mount of Olives. The first Yemenite immigrants who arrived in 1882 lived there in hideous conditions, some in caves.

[21]   See Jehoash Hirshberg, *Paul Ben-Haim, his Life and Works* (Jerusalem, 1990), Chapter 9.

[22]   Bracha Zefira, *Many Voices* (Ramat Gan, 1978), 21–2.

[23]   Jehoash Hirshberg, 'Alexander U. Boskovitch and the Quest for an Israeli National Musical Style', *Studies in Contemporary Jewry*, 9 (Jerusalem and Oxford, 1993).

Aharon to occasionally merge his ensemble with the Studio Players so that the 'ūd and the qānūn were heard together with violin, flute, and cello. Aharon even experimented with harmonization, overcoming the difficulty of the intonation of the three-quarter tone by assigning the third degree in maqām rast and the second in maqām bayāt to the Arabic instruments while the western instruments harmonized them by the first degree.[24] The limited resources of the small radio station, however, did not allow for the spread of the idea into public performances and it remained an isolated experiment.

With the exception of Ezra Aharon's official ensemble, the practice of Arabic instruments remained compartmentalized within the communities of Oriental Jews and among the Arabs. The curriculum of the small music schools (the first of which opened in Jaffa in 1910) was strictly based on the central European model of individual instrumental lessons with most youngsters taking the piano and the violin, and adjacent instruction in solfeggio and music theory. The Palestine Conservatoire in Jerusalem (founded 1933) was the largest and most comprehensive, with classes of varying size for nearly all western instruments. Ezra Aharon was appointed to teach the 'ūd, but there was no interest among serious students.

With no available players of Arabic instruments capable of playing new music, ideologically motivated composers turned to emulation of such instruments on the piano, as, for example, the first movement of Boskovitch's Semitic Suite and the heterophonic texture of Wolpe's 'If it be my fate'. (see Music Examples 1 and 2)

The model established during the Yishuv was so powerful that it has persisted virtually to the present day, despite the overwhelming and frequent social and cultural upheavals which have taken place since the establishment of the State of Israel in 1948. Internal politics repeatedly exploited the east-west dichotomy. Successful ensembles combining western and eastern instruments have appeared in the field of popular music, but they have remained in the minority. So have the sparse attempts at combining eastern soloists with western ensembles in art music, such as Mark Kopytman's highly successful orchestral piece Memory, which opens and closes with a traditional monophonic rendition of a genuine Yemenite song performed by the Yemenite singer Gila Bashari. The Musicology department at the Hebrew university has established a workshop of non-European music, consisting mostly of a gamelan ensemble, but its orientation remains academic. The professional performing schools, such as the two Academies of Music, have not followed suit, and plans for a western-type institutionalised school for Arabic music were entangled in ideological and personal politics and did not get off the ground. Compartmentalization has so far retained the upper hand.

---

[24]   A recorded interview with Prof. Amnon Shiloah, 1981. I am indebted to Prof. Shiloah for allowing me to use the valuable material. Maqām rast starts with a tetrachord of one whole tone followed by two 3/4 tones. Maqām bayāt begins with two 3/4 tones followed by a whole tone. They are most prevalent in Arabic music.

Music Example 1   Alexander U. Boskovitch, Semitic Suite

Music Example 2   Stefan Wolpe, *If it be my fate*

Musical Performance,
1997, Vol. 1, Part 2, pp. 15–33
Reprints available directly from the publisher
Photocopying permitted by license only

Ḥavurot Hazemer in Israel

A Unique Sociomusicological Phenomenon

Natan Shahar

The phenomenon of 'Song Groups' can be seen as a socio-cultural phenomenon that is characteristic of Israeli society in the 1980s. A retrospective view of Israeli society indicates that this is part of the 'Community Singing' movement which since the beginning of the century has been the most distinct characteristic of Israeli society.

According to a study of Song Groups, conducted between 1991 and 1993, a Song Group can be defined as: a group of men and women between the age of 33 and 55 who have similar ethnic backgrounds and mentalities and who are fond of songs; who meet regularly for the study and performance of Hebrew songs with an instructor and musical accompaniment. In 1991 there were over 700 Song Groups of this kind active in Israel taking part in a wide variety of social and cultural activities, and participating successfully in song conferences and international festivals around the world.

KEY WORDS *Ḥavurot Hazemer, Kibbutz,* Song Groups.

Although *Ḥavurot Hazemer,* 'Song Companies', analogous to the French *'Les compagnons de la chanson* have existed for several decades, no attempt has been made until now to study the phenomenon. This article is the first discussion of a number of initial findings I have reached as a result of my research in the field during the period from 1991 to 1993.

1. Community Singing (Sing-Alongs, *Shira be–tzibur*) as the background for the growth of *Ḥavurot Hazemer.*

In view of the basic assumption that musical life and creativity are a direct outgrowth of social life and an aspect of socialized expression one may consider the phenomenon of *Ḥavurot Hazemer* one form of the development of the 'songs of *Eretz-Yisrael'* in general and of community singing in particular.[1] Since the beginning of Zionist immigration, but above all from the period of the second wave of immigration (1904–1914) and the third (1919–1923)[2], community singing began to embody one of the characteristics of society in pre-State days and then later in the State of Israel as well.[3] Indeed in the recorded reminiscences of

---

[1]   This material, up to the year 1949, was discussed extensively by Natan Shahar in *The Songs of Eretz Israel from 1920 to 1950*: Socio-musical and Musical Aspects (Dissertation in Hebrew), Hebrew University, Jerusalem, 1989.

[2]   From the end of the 18th century onwards *Eretz Israel* was settled in stages. It is customary to view these settlement stages in accordance with the waves of Zionist immigration (*'aliya*) from the European countries. The first *'aliya* was from 1882–1903: the second from 1904–1914; the third from 1919–1923: the fourth from 1924–1928 and the fifth from 1929–1948.

[3]   Until the establishment of the State of Israel (15.5.48) the community in the country was called the population or Society of *Eretz Israel* (thereafter, population).

people who came with these immigration waves one finds hundreds of references to community singing. They all describe it as a social activity which starts when a few people gather together, whether for a specific event (meeting, party, lecture, memorial, etc.) or simply to pass the time. Either during or at the end of the gathering the group would begin to sing spontaneously and whoever was present at the time would join in, whether they had participated in the activity or not. None of these many descriptions indicates who initiated or directed the sing along.

Some writers include a description of the *Hora* and Rondo danced to the accompaniment of these songs, pointing out specific characteristics of an egalitarian society in the first stages of social crystalization. During the 30s and 40s community singing continued to be at the heart of every event, but from then on a 'leader' was added. His job was to choose those songs most appropriate for any given occasion. Another reason for his presence was the need to keep the singers together and to maintain order, particularly at large gatherings attended by mixed groups of adults, youths and children. It should be noted that in most cases the leader was the school singing teacher: at a later stage he also became the conductor of the local choir. Eventually young teachers began to play the accordion to accompany the singing.

Community singing may also be considered an important social factor as it was the basic element of the *Eretz-Israeli* celebration and the source from which the voluntary singing groups grew – the amateur choirs and *Havurot Hazemer*.[4]

The various forms of group singing continued to be a cultural characteristic of Israeli society in the years following the War of Independence (1948). It became further entrenched during the 60s when the impact of nostalgic outbursts found intensified expression in community singing of Israeli songs which had been composed prior to the establishment of the State. Things reached the point where the term 'Songs of *Eretz Israel*' became semantically accepted in contexts that did not always conform to the historical and musical significance of the term. The cultural establishment's recognition of this activity is apparent from the incorporation of community singing into state affairs such as 'The Festival of Songs and Ballads' that became the official closing event of Independence Day festivities.

2. Development of *Havurot Hazemer* in Israel – Historical Survey From the historical point of view, *Havurot Hazemer* began to emerge in the second half of the fifties. The *Kibbutz* movement – which had begun in the early twenties – served as fertile ground for this development. Until after the War of Independence in 1948 almost all the older *kibbutzim* had mixed a-cappella choirs made up of *Kibbutz* members. The choir, generally under the direction of the local school music teacher, would meet after work for weekly rehearsals.

The choir was expected to participate actively in all *Kibbutz* events (*Shabbat* ceremonies, seasonal holidays, commemoration of Settlement Day, etc.). It is worthy of note that as compared with anywhere else, the *Kibbutz* offered a choir maximum opportunities to appear before an audience. As a cultural activity encompassing several dozen members, the choir also conformed to the social policies of the *Kibbutzim* and of the *Kibbutz* movement as a whole, whose policy was to include the maximum number of members in local cultural groups.

---

[4]   An extensive discussion of this subject can be found in my pamphlet: *The Songs of Eretz Israel and the Jewish National Fund*; published by the *Keren Kayemet* (Jewish National Fund), 1994.

The fifties was the last period in which amateur choirs flourished in *Kibbutzim* and Local Councils. Toward the end of the decade a sharp decline was perceptible in the number of choirs in *Kibbutzim*, cities and villages. This decline can be explained by a number of interrelated elements (at this point it should be pointed out that one of the results of the drop in choir activities was the growth of *Ḥavurot Hazemer*). The reasons for the decline were:

(i) artistic standards were not high enough; they were, after all, amateur choirs. This was also the reason given for not including them in the *Zimriyah* (song-fests) held in Israel during those years.[5]

(ii) reduced intensity of activity which expressed itself primarily in decreased readiness on the part of the members (and potential participants) to appear regularly for rehearsals. This can be explained by the constant repetition of the same repertory since most of the occasions on which the choir appeared were in celebration of local holidays when the same repertory was used over and over again. In addition the aimless and unrewarding nature of routine choir work, sometimes with a veteran choir leader with nothing new to offer, became uninteresting. One of the inevitable results was that a significant number of the local amateur choirs ceased functioning. Something more dynamic, innovative, and attractive seemed to be required. The reduction in the number of amateur choirs, together with the reduction in the number of participants in those that remained, immediately generated two significant results: the establishment of large amalgamated choirs of the *Kibbutz* movement, which drew on all those with vocal ability who wanted to sing in artistic choirs, such as The *Ihud* choir (1955); the *Kibbutz Hameuḥad* choir (1952), the *Kibbutz Ha-Artzi* choir (1951). When these choirs were established and functioning, it became possible to raise the musical standard by, among other things, improving the participants' voices by vocal training: raising the musical standard of the individuals; widening the repertory; introducing choir leaders and music instructors. The existence of these centralized choirs also suggested a solution for all those sworn a-cappella choir-lovers in *Kibbutzim* who were the hard core of singers at that time. In addition, a new sphere of collective singing emerged for dozens of small groups, each of which numbered 10 to 25 male and female participants. The names used to describe these groups, other than choir, were *Lahaqa Qolit* (Vocal troupe), *Lahaqat Hazemer* (Song Troupe) These were, in effect, the first *Ḥavurot Hazemer* – Song Companies.

The transition from permanent amateur choirs in *kibbutzim* to ad hoc choirs and other kinds of vocal groups in the *kibbutzim* also found expression in a change in the set-up of the groups' conductors and managers. As already stated, these had been *kibbutz* members and singing teachers in local schools who usually lacked a full musical education or training in conducting. Since they were music-lovers and were needed, musical activities were put in their hands. One-off extension courses were organized to help them in a variety of musical fields, including choir- leading. These courses were organized by the Music Section of the General Federation of Labor's Cultural Center, and it was this that was largely responsible for the fact that the choirs so resembled one another in respect to sound, staging and repertory.

It was at this time (the second half of the 50s) that the various army troupes became among the most original socio-musical representatives of Israeli society.

---

[5]   The *Zimriyah* started at a convention of world-wide Jewish choirs in which a number of amateur choirs from Israel also took part.

Outstanding examples were the *Nahal* troupe (founded in 1951) and that of the Central Area HQ (founded in 1953). These troupes imbued 'Israeli song' with a new, youthful, more dynamic image. Although they were formed for the purpose of entertainment, these army groups stressed the musical side, and introduced a previously unheard indigenous sound to Israeli songs. These new songs were written by Israel's finest composers and poets, some of whom even started their careers writing for army troupes. At first the instrumental accompaniment for army ensembles, each of which contained from 10 to 14 boys and girls, was based on the accordion. The appellation Song Troupe also achieved wide-spread popularity thanks to the army troupe.

At the end of the 1950s the French *Les compagnons de la chanson* arrived in Israel for a series of appearances. The translation of its name to *Havurot Hazemer Hatzarfati* – which gave rise to the name *Havurot Hazemer* – Song Company – quickly caught on and became identified with the small vocal groups that began to form during that time in labor settlements, cities and villages. The name was readily accepted. The word *havurah* – circle – has quite a positive connotation in Israeli society, the word *hevruta* is also accepted among certain circumscribed traditional study groups. As society in *Eretz Israel* was evolving, the various forms derived from the root *Haver* – *compagnon* in French, *companion* or *circle* in English – acquired the meaning of a group with a special common interest.

Music Section of the *Histadrut* Cultural Center

Central Body for choirs and *Havurot Hazemer*

The proliferation of amateur choirs early in the fifties is implicit in the abundance of written material that was published for them by the Music Section of the *Histadrut* Cultural Center and either distributed free of charge or sold for a nominal sum to all choir directors in *kibbutzim*. The material was also sent to the cultural committees of the *kibbutzim* and to those active in cultural work on the Labor Councils of cities and villages, to teachers of singing in urban schools sponsored by the Labour Party and to the singing teachers in *kibbutz* schools.

It should be pointed out that at that time the Cultural Center of the General Labor Federation took care of everything connected with musical activity in the *kibbutz* movement, with particular emphasis on fostering the amateur choirs; it was for this that the Music Section had been established. For most of the years of its existence people from the labor settlements headed this section. The Section's activities naturally expanded to include choirs then being formed in cities and villages, most of which were founded and maintained by the municipal labor councils. An examination of the material published by the Music Section reveals the unmistakable process of transition from the Art Song of the Renaissance and Baroque periods, through the East-European folk song, arranged for mixed amateur choirs, (in the style of F. Jode),[6] through the *Eretz Israeli* folk song arranged artistically, and ending with popular Israeli songs.

---

[6]   Fritz Jode, a German musician who did a great deal to acquaint the masses with art music, by simplifying and popularizing it as well as by introducing games and entertainment. He had an important influence on musicians and choir leaders. His methods and systems had many protagonists in Israel, including Yehuda Sharet.

Beginnings of *Havurot Hazemer*

In the early 60s a number of *Havurot Zemer* were formed in the larger cities, the forerunners of many such groups that arose thereafter. Among them were *Shiru Shir* (Sing a Song), formed in Beit Hillel in Jerusalem under the direction of Meir Harnik, and the Beit Rothschild (Rothschild House) group in Haifa, directed by Ephi Netzer. In addition there was the oldest of such groups – the *Gevatron* that originated in Kvutzat Geva' in the Jezreel Valley – and then there were dance groups that interspersed their dances with Hebrew songs (primarily the 'Carmon Troupe and a dance group formed by the Hebrew University of Jerusalem). These groups, and the ad hoc youth groups that were sent to the Festival of Democratic Youth held in the Communist Bloc countries during the 50s, marked the inception of the distinctive Israeli style and type of repertory that became widespread when the *Havurot Hazemer* arose later. This repertoire contained Hebrew folksongs and songs of *Eretz Israel*.

The interpretation of these songs ranged from singing in unison accompanied by a harmonic and/or melodic instrument (usually accordion, flute/clarinet and Arab drum) to two kinds of two-part responses: one, males and females separately: the other with one part based on thirds, the other on sixths. From the standpoint of vocal texture the sound of these *havurot* can be characterized by a male solo responding to a female solo, with an answering chorus (a kind of response) and between one group and another (a kind of antiphony). (see Music Examples 1, 2 and 3)

Instruments typically used for accompaniment were the piano, and/or accordion and the contra-bass. To these were added the flute, clarinet, bassoon, trumpet which were the basis of the ensemble put together by Nahum Heiman for The Gilboa Quintet in the Jezreel Valley during the fifties. An additional instrument was the Arab drum which offered the drummer relatively varied possibilities: he could use his finger-tips, entire hand, soft inner palm, or any of these combined. The range of tone was also extremely rich: beating in the center of the drum head, on the external frame, or any place between the center and the rim.

Among the various groups the massive radiophonic presence of Jerusalem's *Shiru Shir* was conspicuous. This can be explained by the fact that Meir Harnik, its leader, worked for the department of folk music of *Kol Yisrael*, the government radio station in Jerusalem.

A significant change occurred in the groups' sounds with the establishment in 1962 of *Havurat Renanim*, (Happy Singers' Company) led by Gil Aldema (also a programmer for (*Kol Yisrael*)). Composed of 8 to 12 men and women, this group was formed not to appear before audiences, but to record songs that were missing from the radio's collections – for which there was an increasing demand in view of the waves of nostalgia then sweeping over Israeli society.

From the musical standpoint *Havurat Renanim* was outstanding for its vocal arrangements and instrumental accompaniments. The arrangements were for 3 or 4 voices, with a relatively broad range, accompanied by bass guitar and two or three wood-winds (usually flute and clarinet, alternating with the voices in thirds and sixths.) The members of this group all belonged to the *Rinnat* choir and were trained to a high level of a-cappella singing in a professional choir. This enabled them to perform Gil Aldema's special arrangements which were in a way a combination of traditional polyphonic and homophonic textures with harmonic

הַלְלוּיָה

HALLELUYAH

from PSALM 150

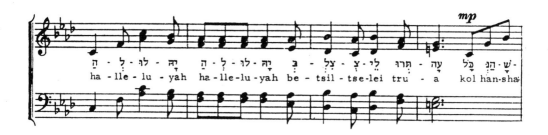

Music Example 1 *Halleluyah*: Division of voices: two-parts, men and women with limited range
(1 octave). Part of a song in oriental folk style. The symmetrical structure of the tune facilitates
alternating voices.

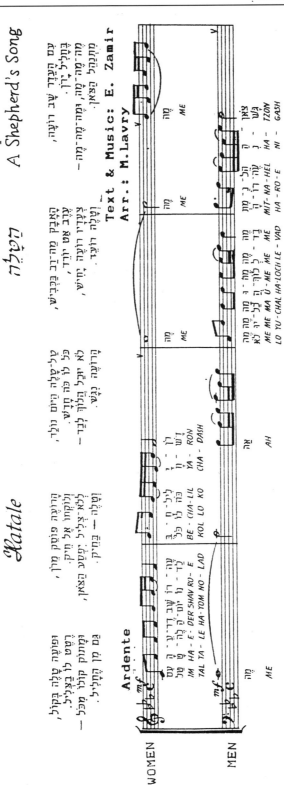

Music Example 2 *A Shepherd's Song*: An arrangement of a shepherd's song written during the 1950s. The shepherd songs of that period tried to imitate the sound of the shepherd and the simultaneous bleating of sheep. The drawn-out sound sung alternately by the men and then the women is on the onomatopoetic syllable "me-h-h" reminiscent of a sheep's bleating.

Ahavat Hadasa expresses, allegorically, a yearning for salvation.

Music Example 3 *Ahavat Hadasa*: The original melody (a folk song) is sung by male voices. An independent melodic line written for the women opens the song. This melody does not resemble the original one, nor does it refer to it. Singing it separately enables the use of the Doric mode. Using it in the opening part of the song seems to create a new work. The entrance of the males singing the original melody as the females repeat the previous melody line creates a new pattern and additional effect. The pattern sounds polyphonious – like a kind of free-organum. The original melody is in Bb (Si-Flat Major). The two lines of melody create interesting harmonization in a song of oriental ethnic origin.

and melodic instrumental accompaniment as outlined above. (see Music Example 4) The songs of this group were heard very frequently, which did a great deal to entrench their sound among those devoted to Israeli songs.

Shuru Habitu Wu (Look how great is this day) expresses the happiness of working on the Land.

Music Example 4 *Shuru Habitu Wu:* Here we have the beginning of an arrangement for men and women. *Havurot Hazemer* accompanied by two melodic instruments: flute and clarinet, guitar, and bass. Any percussion instrument – usually drums – can be added. Each of the groups divides into two parts (Bars 7–8; 9–10). The melody is accompanied by the wind instruments and the guitar and the bass create a harmonic and rythmic framework.

Music Example 4 (continued)

During this same period government radio stations also began to broadcast the *Gevatron* accompanied by the Gilboa Quintet. Their songs became popular request numbers on song programs and they also 'captured the Israeli street'. One of the first *Ḥavurot Hazemer* formed during the sixties was *Zammarèi Aviv* (Spring singers) which later became *Adam le Adam* (Person-to-Person), directed and led by Yaakov Hollander. According to him, the idea of the *Havurot Hazemer* format came to him even before the name itself became popular, after he had auditioned candidates for a choir to be established by the Ramat Gan Labor Council: 'After testing and examining the candidates for the choir I saw that I did not really have true choir voices. The girls could reach only as high as Re or Mi in the second octave, whereas a choir needs sopranos that can get at least as high as Sol and La. The boys sang in mid-range, somewhere between baritone and tenor; I did not have a single bass or choir-worthy tenor. In a preliminary discussion they asked that we should not sing the usual choir songs, but rather new Israeli songs from song festivals, army groups, etc. There were no prepared arrangements for the songs they wanted and I myself had to be the arranger. I don't know whether these arrangements would have received a passing grade at the Academy of Music, but the ability to try to perform them, while listening on the spot to their 'ring' and with the immediate possibility of changing the vocal procedures, made it possible for me to achieve the unique sound produced by the choir. The members' readiness to work hard and achieve uniformity all contributed to the immediate success of their appearances. Elsewhere the following was written about the *Renanim* song company: The event – a gathering of musicians in Tel Aviv. Outstanding professionals from Israel and abroad assembled to listen to choir performances. After a number of cantatas and motets *Renanim* came on stage. Thirty young people in colorful attire, without bow-ties, evening gowns or black-bound scores. Some of those present hid yawns; others raised an eyebrow ... At the end of the first song the yawns disappeared ... the experienced musicians became the kind of attentive, curious audience *Renanim* is used to. As the conductors began to leave, one of them said: 'There is no such thing as classical singing or folk singing – there is poor performance and fine performance . . .'

It may be said that these song circles, few at first, created the musical foundation for the many groups that proliferated during the 70s (above all after the *Yom Kippur* War) and the beginning of the 80s (see Figures 1 and 2).

The transition from a-cappella choir to *Havurot Hazemer* can be viewed from another standpoint as well: that of a change in the age of the leaders, the singers, and the devoted audience. The conductors on the one hand had been long-time choir leaders who were unable to change the way they had always worked (with a-cappella choirs), as against the group of young leaders who were more receptive to change, had internalized the rhythms of light music of the fifties and sixties – including the foreign songs – and above all, were willing to innovate. In addition to the age difference, they also lacked the stringent traditions of European choir directors. Then, too, there was the singers' desire for a different repertory, based primarily on familiar Hebrew songs (associated with the pervasive nostalgia), and new songs that were written specially for them. They wanted new Israeli songs in more modern rhythms, (perhaps influenced by foreign songs), as well as other accompanying instruments. The age of the participants in the *Havurot Hazemer* was lower; most of them were in their twenties (after their army service), and they were motivated above all by the desire to sing together.

Most of the new conductors were young composers who had begun to publicize their songs at that very time. Some of these songs were awarded first prize at song festivals and were broadcast frequently. Cultural and official institutions also became interested in community singing and the *Festival of Songs and Ballads*, held in 1965, included community singing as part of its program.

An important aspect of these developments was the audience – and it received the *Havurot Hazemer* very well. After the end of the Six Day War (1967) further changes took place within these *Havurot*, and there was an increased demand on the part of potential participants who sought an enjoyable socio-cultural framework. Glee Clubs (both one-off and regular) also arose as the popularity of Israeli songs crested. Community singing became very popular at that time, and *Havurot Hazemer* would be invited to participate: such occasions offered them natural platforms. Participants in the glee clubs were devotees who wanted to sing Hebrew songs – and at the same time hear new arrangements. The inauguration of the government television channel after the Six Day War and the more formal institutionalization of *Havurot Hazemer* contributed much to their popularity.

Havurot Hazemer: **Second Period**

Quantitatively, the number of *havurot* grew steadily, alongside the many glee clubs. At the beginning of the 70s, and even more during the 80s, the electric organ (later the synthesizer, the midi, and the computer) came into use as a basic instrument to accompany the various *Havurot Hazemer*. This much simplified the instrumental accompaniment required, both for public appearances and for rehearsals. From the standpoint of rehearsals the need for a piano decreased; performances, too, were no longer dependent upon a piano which was replaced by the electric organ, an available, mobile instrument. The use of the organ, and then

Figure 1   *Havurot Hazemer* 'Kramim'

Figure 2   Part of *Havurot Hazemer* 'Kramim'

the synthesizer and computer, simplified the preparatory work for a significant number of leaders of *Havurot* who made their own instrumental arrangements. Henceforth it sufficed to write the melody and simply indicate the basic chords above the notes in the usual manner.

This had other implications as well: it hastened the rate of replacement of conductors and leaders for the *Havurot Hazemer*. Old-timers were unable to master the electronic instruments and exploit them to the full, which introduced dozens of young people into the circle of conductors and leaders, people who knew and were completely at home in the world of electronic music.

During the seventies additional progress was made in the *Havurot* primarily from an institutional point of view, and also from budgetary and stylistic standpoints. In March 1976 the first Assembly of national song groups was held at *kibbutz* Gan Shmuel. It was organized by the *Histadrut's* Music section of the Center for Culture and Education, together with the music divisions of the Federation of *Kibbutz* Movements. Forty long-established, permanent groups and *Havurot Hazemer* appeared, most of them from the *Kibbutz* movement, the rest from city and village Labor Councils. At this assembly one could study at close range what was special about the sound, staging etc. of the *Havurot Hazemer*.

This was the first time one could clearly see and analyse not only what it was that essentially differentiated the choir performances from those of the *Havurot Hazemer*, but also the differences between one *Havurah* and another. But more than that, one could see that the differences between one *Havurah* and another involved widely diverse parameters, not only in the quality of voice and performance, but also in the form of performance, staging, sound, the manner of constructing the program, musical arrangements, vocal texture and the texture of the accompanying instruments, the way the stage was utilized, and the exploitation of electronic effects.

Unlike the artistic choir with its many years of tradition and accepted standards, the *Havurot Hazemer* was a new body in which the standard was determined by the available material. In other words, the criteria for *Havurot Hazemer* was established in accordance with the manner and form of performance, the use of amplifying equipment and the preparation and presentation of instrumental accompaniments. Another element was the reaction of the audience. The fact that each *Havurah* performed exclusively the arrangements prepared by its leader also brought about some absurd situations: in the course of the years some of these absurdities even became norms (such as performing with simultaneous playbacks).

The 'arrangers' license assumed by the musical directors resulted in the creation of some unique sounds.

Ḥavurot Hazemer: **the Peak Years of the Eighties**

In 1982 the Arad Festival was held for the first time: it was a festival of *Havurot Hazemer*. Organized by the Local Council and the Government Tourist Office, the festival was sponsored by several hotels and industrial plants of the region. The administrative director, who had originally conceived the idea, was Zacharia Liraz of Be'ersheva. Ephi Netzer, leader of Haifa's *Beit Rothschild Havurot Hazemer* and one of the best known conductors of community singing in Israel, was the artistic director.

The staff viewed the festival as an opportunity for lovers of Hebrew songs to meet, and as a platform on which song groups and *Havurot Hazemer* – the backbone of the program – could become mutually acquainted. In the course of time the Arad Festival became a magnet for secondary school students (from 14 to 19), who were attracted mainly by the popular rock performances. In just a few years the *Havurot Hazemer* became a necessary burden at Arad and occupied an ever smaller place in the festival. There was virtually no audience for their appearances, with the exception of the performers' family and friends. Those that succeeded in drawing a crowd (as attested by tickets sold) could be counted on both hands. They began to stage their performances outdoors and rarely charged admission. Consequently, the festival changed from *Havurot Hazemer* to Rock groups, with the type and age of the audience gradually changing as well.

The Arad Festival in 1982 marked the highest point achieved by the *Havurot Hazemer* which I believe continued for another 6 or 7 years. During those years the number of such groups reached some 600. If we take an average of 22 to 24 participants in each company, we arrive at a figure of some 13,200 to 14,400 singers who came to at least one rehearsal a week (not counting the special rehearsals and performances).

During its early years Israeli television made frequent use of the large *Havurot Hazemer* and thereby contributed much to raising the sound quality. For most television appearances a great deal of preparatory work was necessary, including recording the songs before filming, usually in specially equipped recording studios. When the films were shown it was possible to hear the fruits of the studio work, which facilitated critical assessment of the vocal quality. When the group was being filmed, emphasis shifted to form and apparel and the performance, therefore, showed the *Havurah* at its best. An appearance on the government television channel during prime time – on Friday nights or at the end of *Shabbat* – was a tacit confirmation, so to speak, of the high level and fine quality of the *Havurah*. When twinning between Israeli cities and cities abroad (primarily in Western European countries) was being enthusiastically pursued, *Havurot Hazemer* were an important part of Israel's good-will delegations: they were often the first organized groups to be sent as representatives of local authorities and they appeared as such in public. They returned home flushed with success and new experiences.

The Current Picture and Initial Research Findings

During the years 1991–1993 I carried out a comprehensive study of *Havurot Hazemer* from various sociomusical angles. In the course of the study questionnaires were distributed, the groups were observed during rehearsals and performances, interviews were held with the singers, musical directors, administrators and representatives of bodies that finance the groups, as well as with people who constituted the audience.

On the basis of the data accumulated it is now possible to answer several questions and postulate a number of conclusions with respect to the *Havurot Hazemer* that were active at the beginning of the 90s.

A)   What is a *Ḥavurat Hazemer*?

A precise, all-inclusive definition has not yet been forthcoming although hundreds of such groups exist in Israel. Hundreds of people, including musical directors, singers, administrators, etc. were asked this question in writing and orally and on the basis of the answers received, one may attempt to define *Ḥavurot Hazemer* as follows:

> A group of people possessing a common origin and similar mentality who love Hebrew songs, assemble regularly to learn and perform Hebrew songs and ballads under the leadership of a conductor, with accompanying instruments.

This definition, which includes 7 different components, applies to 85% of the *Ḥavurot* that were studied in the course of this research. Each of these components has different sub-components which when combined in various ways produce the distinctive aspects of the various *Ḥavurot Hazemer*. An example: the 'group of people' can include 8 to 35 participants; the makeup of the group men and women; or only men and only women; the ages range from 21 to 66, and so on. Definition of age-range excluded many otherwise typical *Ḥavurot Hazemer* from the scope of the study. Examples are: young *Ḥavurot* called 'Youth of Tel Aviv', 'Youth of Herzlia', 'Youth of Ahuza' etc. – such groups were very common at the beginning of the 90s. A number of other groups excluded from the research were those functioning in retirement and old-age homes.

Another component of the definition: 'with accompanying instruments' has sub-components such as type of instrument – from a piano and/or guitar, to a full orchestra, synthesizer and/or computer, all the way to a tape-recorded accompaniment.

Each of the groups studied in the course of the research had been functioning for at least two years. The group that had been functioning for the longest time and had a 75% turnover in membership, had been established in 1968.

B)   How the *Ḥavurot Hazemer* were formed and maintained

Most of the groups included in the study were established during the 1980s, a few in the 70s or before. The more typical ways in which they came into being were:

(i) by emerging from a glee club: the desire of a group of people to sing together which led to regular cultural gatherings, the basis of which was community singing of new and old songs, followed by the formation of a glee club with a conductor. Such clubs were sponsored by some public institution such as a local or regional council, a *Kibbutz* cultural committee, etc. The singers would also consolidate socially 'over coffee and cake' and then eventually evolve into a *Ḥavurot Hazemer* – a close-knit nucleus, united first and foremost by the idea of singing together.

(ii) as a result of some special celebration: a central part of the established pattern for celebrations and other events in the *Kibbutz*, including jubilee celebrations, was always a choir or group of singers organized specially for the occasion. A professional would be invited to instruct the singers. There were intensive preparations and rehearsals (a number of meetings a week for several hours each), which in the course of time became a special experience for those who participated. When the event was over this body continued to function under the same musical director, with a smaller number of participants.

(iii) as an extension of Centers for Culture, Youth and Sport, Clubhouses, and Community Centers: the establishment during the 70s of community centers in development towns and municipal suburbs throughout the country gave strong impetus to the formation of many additional *Havurot Hazemer*. Other community buildings that took local needs into consideration built rooms – in addition to auditoriums with an average of 300–500 seats – for creative cultural activities, including rehearsal rooms for theatre groups or song circles. Some of these rooms were equipped with acoustic ceilings. The presence of a *Havurot Hazemer* in these centers facilitated the eventual establishment of an overall organizational frame-work and encouraged the institutions' central administration to function in special ways. A similar process took place in the formation of such *Havurot Hazemer* in Labor Councils, *Na'amat* and *Mofet* clubs – municipally based cultural frameworks of national workers' organizations.

(iv) in large work-places: during the 70s, and even more so during the 80s, *Havurot Hazemer*/choirs were established in large work places such as the Electric Company, Aeronautics Industry, Discount Bank, Bank Leumi, Teachers' Federa-tion, Tel Aviv Municipality, etc. The groups were financed by the work-place which paid for the musical director's salary, costume/uniforms, and even subsidized the participants by paying overtime for the time spent at rehearsals and performances.

(v) by private initiative: this method of establishing *Havurot Hazemer* was widespread, mainly during the second half of the 80s. The establishment of such a group was usually the initiative of a single person who had no connection with any institution, public or municipal body, but was obsessed with the idea. Following announcements in the local press potential participants would gather together and the group would be formed. The fact that a number of *Havurot Hazemer* were formed in this way indicates that some people could not find their place in any of the already-existing groups. Unlike the *Havurot* formed in the more usual ways, the members of these privately established groups had to pay all expenses from their own pockets – which sometimes meant that the activity was short-lived.

Costs and Expenditure of *Havurot Hazemer*

With the exception of those groups formed by private initiative, all the others were under the auspices of a public and/or municipal body. Such dependency stemmed from the basic obligation of the groups to pay the musical director's salary which in 1993 was a minimum of $500, a small sum for travel expenses, for musical arrangements, VAT, etc. Some of the *Havurot* had to improve their performances and staging which meant employing a choreographer and stage-director. Many *Havurot* did not use the musical instructor as an accompanist, which meant additional payment was required for the accompaniment and/or a separate payment for preparing a recorded play-back. Additional expenses include the preparation of special costumes and other small outlays, such as for hot or cold drinks during rehearsals. All these are the regular expenses occasioned by the year's activities. In addition there were extra rehearsals, appearances that necessitated additional payments such as transportation to and from performances, etc. Income for these groups is minimal: in most cases all payments come from the public bodies that support the activities such as the Local Council, Regional Council, *Kibbutz*, Center for Culture, Youth and Sport, Labor Councils, *Na'amat*, etc.

The Repertory: the repertory includes Hebrew songs from all periods, starting with *Ḥibbat Tzion* (1882). As the years passed, but particularly from the 70s onward, the *Ḥavurot Hazemer* began to increase their repertoires: sometimes a programme would be based on an individual composer or poet (names or particular places – the Emek, Kineret, the sea. Programmes would be based on the songs of well-known singers (names), groups (names) or there would be songs in Russian. Sometimes presentation of a country's songs of this kind contributed much to the treasury of the country's songs either by making new contributions or by adding something new to a given song through performing it in a novel arrangement. The repertory is usually fixed by the musical director who sometimes consults with a committee of the *Ḥavurot Hazemer* or with a representative of the body that holds the purse-strings.

Characteristics: at the end of 1993 there were 250 functioning *Ḥavurot Hazemer* that corresponded with the above definition (from the beginning of the study in 1991 until its conclusion, several groups ceased functioning for varying reasons). The findings show that some 70% of the members are women, some 30% men. Of course, some groups are differently constituted, such as the all-male *Ḥavurah* from Afikim, or the all-female group *Benot Mesillot*. The average age groups are those born between 1941 and 1958, with a sprinkling of some older or younger participants. Some 85% of participants are *Ashkenazi*: fewer than 15% originated in the Arab-speaking countries (or their parents were from those countries); 37% of the members of the *Ḥavurot* have an academic education, the men accounting for 49%, the women for 25%. Most of the men are in the free professions such as teachers, engineers, etc. 34% of the women are teachers, 10% are homemakers: some 57% are in other professions fashion, cosmetics, medicine, etc. Number of years as members: most of those participating have sung in choirs and/or *Ḥavurot Hazemer* for 7 or more years. Musical education: in their youth some 34% of the males and some 46% of the women learned to play a musical instrument – a total of about 43% have varying levels of musical experience. Ability to read music: some 21% read music well; about 30% can do so to some degree; about 49% cannot read music at all. This subject has arisen a number of times in discussions held socially in various *Ḥavurot Hazemer*, particularly as it affects the level of the group and the better utilization of rehearsal time. Among other things, it has been suggested that instruction be given in reading music. Only 38% of those who participated expressed willingness to take such lessons, most expressing objection to the similarity with choirs. The subject of voice training (over and above warming up) elicited similar reactions.

Ḥavurot Hazemer as a social framework: most of these groups hold rehearsals on the same day every week. Such a rehearsal usually last two hours. As can be seen, most of the *Ḥavurot* sit in a circle or semi-circle, with the leader standing or sitting next to the instrument, if he himself accompanies the singing, which is most usual. Or they may all sit around a large table with the leader at the head. The participants usually have permanent places, according to the parts they sing. This seating order also creates a coordinated sociometric pattern when it comes to choosing the *Havurah's* committee. Few of these groups sit in the straight rows usually formed by choirs. For those groups that prepare stage productions the rehearsal room becomes a sort of performance platform and rehearsals are conducted accordingly. With *Havurot* who give static performances, the seating order of the singers is sometimes similar to that in which they stand. At least 15 minutes of each rehearsal is devoted to a coffee break, held at the half-way mark. As the years passed such tea or coffee breaks, designed to develop social relations, have become traditional. All participants take turns bringing cake. Sometimes the *Havurah's* committee or administrative body utilize the recess for formalities; then again the entire recess may be used for social purposes and the formalities are discussed at the beginning of the second hour of rehearsals.

Some 64% of the members responded that they meet with other members of the *Havurah* between once and ten times a month, outside the framework of rehearsals. Others noted that most of their friends were from the *Havurot Hazemer*. About 84% expressed their desire to expand the existing social framework and even offered suggestions, such as increasing the recess-time, and/or holding social get-togethers, and/or attending performances together, and/or going on trips together, in this country and abroad. It should be noted that many of these *Havurot* have gone abroad together, either as delegations to twin-cities or on a personal basis. Further social coherence has resulted from such trips in which spouses also participated.

Almost all participants in these groups relate to the *Havurot Hazemer* as a social framework; for some of them it is their only social framework. They are careful never to miss a rehearsal or performance. Others see this not only as a social framework but an artistic one as well. On the other hand, the cessation or disintegration of a group is usually based on social disagreements which have even motivated members to join other vocal groups. If the disintegration was against a musical background it has usually brought about a change in the musical director.

At the performances themselves one can also find elements that testify to and reinforce social activity: some try to travel together to and from a performance. Arranging the stage (moving and placing equipment) is usually done collectively. In presenting the singers it is customary to give first names and add their professions, such as 'Yehuda the physician', 'Tzippy the teacher'.

The Musical Directors: One of the basic and central functions within the *Havurot Hazemer* as a musical body is fulfilled by the musical director who prepares his group for a high-level musical presentation. From the research it emerges that in forming a new *Havurot* the musical director is chosen by a representative of the body that finances the project and under whose auspices the group has been formed. This is usually a representative of the cultural department. In the older *Havurot Hazemer*, when the need arose to change the musical director, a committee of members of the *Havurah* was formed to bring recommendations to the supporting body.

During the 80s the proliferation of *Havurot Hazemer* created an increased demand for conductors and musical directors. This created a situation where on the one hand a single leader worked with several groups (usually from 2 to 6), and on the other many inadequately trained amateurs began to enter the field. Most of the musical directors were born during the fifties, and have only had a limited musical education. Very few are graduates of the Academy of Music, although many went through the Training School for music teachers. Others come from an army background, having worked with army troupes. But a significant number lack all musical knowledge, have not attended courses nor have they had any private lessons. Most of them are of European origin, which explains the minimal treatment of oriental material in the repertories of the *Ḥavurot Hazemer*.

Musical Performance,
1997, Vol. 1, Part 2, pp. 35–49
Reprints available directly from the publisher
Photocopying permitted by license only

The Performance of Arab Music in Israel

Suheil Radwan

There were few Arab musicians within the Arab communities following the establishment of the State of Israel, though some musical activities occurred from time to time. In the 1950s an important role was played by immigrant musicians from Iraq, and in the 1960s by those who arrived from Egypt. In the following decades improvements in education and the opening of the Arab music department at the Rubin Conservatory in Haifa produced a new generation of musicians. A renaissance was experienced in schools, clubs, and cultural and community centres throughout the country and music activities flourished; festivals were held and there were radio and TV programmes.

KEY WORDS   Immigrant Jewish musicians from Iraq and Egypt, Music education, the Rubin Conservatory in Haifa, the Radio Orchestra in Tel Aviv, the Arab Music Orchestra in Haifa, Young Arab composers.

Before the British Mandate regime ended in 1948 there were many Arab musicians active in Galilee, especially in Haifa and Nazareth, and also in Jerusalem, Ramalla, and Jaffa. In the last decade Ibrahim Bathish played an important role at the music club he founded in Haifa and many of his graduates, considered among the best musicians, continued to perform in Israel, and later in Lebanon. They included Salim Ḥilu, a distinguished teacher at the Beirut Conservatoire who has had many books published and Ḥalim Rumi, a well known composer and performer of *Muwashshaḥāt* (whose daughter Majīda is now considered one of the finest singers in the Arab world) were his pupils.

With the establishment of the State of Israel and during the Jewish – Arab war most Arab musicians left to continue their musical activities in the surrounding countries. However, three Haifa Club graduates remained, Sudki Shukri, a talented musician (he founded a small orchestra in Haifa in 1943 and later received a scholarship to study for a year at the Cairo Conservatoire in 1946) went to Acre, Michael Dermalkonian, of mixed parentage – his father was Armenian and his mother an Arab – studied both Oriental and European music. In 1949, sponsored by the Communist Party, he founded the Ṭalī 'a (Pioneer) choir in Nazareth. The choir was popular and for over 10 years performed regularly at many venues. Its repertoire included Russian songs, which had been translated into Arabic, as well as Arabic national music and folk songs a number of which were arranged in four parts. The Arabic songs were accompanied by traditional Arab instruments. Ḥikmat Shaheen, another Haifa graduate, returned to his native village, Tarshīḥa, in upper Galilee.

The two Israeli broadcasting stations – in Jerusalem and Jaffa – played an important role in broadcasting Arab music, composed, played and sung by local musicians, living in those cities. In Jerusalem the Jewish musician Ezra Aharon, who had immigrated from Iraq, an excellent 'ūd player had been Head of the Iraqi Delegation to the 1932 Cairo Conference.

Iskander Shahtut, who was already at that time an elderly musician, was involved with musical activities at the Latin church. He founded a brass band at the Catholic Club in Nazareth during the British Mandate and continued to direct it and the church choir until his death in the mid-1950s.

During this time European music activities flourished, in private secondary schools in Jerusalem, in the Training College for Girls in Ramalla, and in Catholic and Protestant churches throughout the country.

Developments in 1950s

Sudki Shukri, who had already founded an orchestra in Haifa, in 1952 founded an Arab Music Orchestra in Acre as well as a Center providing instrumental lessons on 'ūd and violin, to which many young men came from considerable distances. At the start the orchestra was obliged to perform without any financial support, but in 1955 the *Histadrut* commenced to sponsor it. The orchestra (some of its members were Jewish immigrants) played all over Israel and many well known Arab and Jewish singers performed with them.

A number of other valuable developments took place throughout the 50s. Hikmat Shaheen played and gave 'ūd and singing lessons to many young people in Tarshīha and this led to a new generation of talented performers being created. Later, in the mid-50s, he moved to Haifa. Maron Ashqar, a good violinist who played in a number of groups, succeeded in forming an Oriental Ensemble at the Catholic club and subsequently at the *Histradrut* Center in Nazareth and then a choir at the Maronite Church which performed both religious and secular songs.

In 1956 Michael Dermalkonian and I started a music class at the Nazareth YMCA. The 12 students had both theoretical and instrumental tuition. At the same time I was conducting two church choirs in Haifa, one in a Protestant church the other an Orthodox church. In the following years we were able to give several concerts.

The Radio Broadcasting Orchestra, the first professional orchestra in Israel was founded in 1957 by Ezra Aharon. The orchestra enriched the repertoire that was being broadcast and encouraged local composers to write songs especially for radio programmes. The personnel for this orchestra were recruited from the best performers from Iraq and Egypt. At this time, during the 50s two small groups that only performed at wedding parties became extremely well known in Nazareth. They were the Abū Khurūj ensemble and a group led by Nakram Farah; quite frequently, on big occasions they would combine. As well as these groups there were many others that played in private houses for the important Arab families.

The Role of Music Education

The Ministry of Education decided that music should become an obligatory subject in all Arab schools and as a result a demand for music teachers was created. I had been fortunate enough to have studied music at the Haifa Conservatory of Music so that in 1951 I was able to become the first music teacher in the Arab sector and teach in three elementary schools in Nazareth. By the end of the 1950s six music teachers had been appointed including Sudki Shukri, Hikmat Shaheen, and Maron

Ashqar. Yusif Khil also taught part-time. He came from a music loving family and was very involved with the Catholic club and the Latin church where he took over the work Iskander Shahtut had started.

Music was taught in Arab schools for one hour a week from the 3rd to the 8th grade. There was no planned curriculum and at the beginning facilities were very poor; there were no song books and lessons were in the main taken by general class teachers. Each of them taught in their own way and this often amounted to little more than teaching a few songs.

The 1960s

In 1962 the Azzam family formed an ensemble, *The House of Art (Beit al–Fann)* in Nazareth. The father, Salim, a wellknown photographer, had played *'ūd* in Haifa from the time of the Mandate; his wife played the 'cello, his elder son, Nabil, played the violin, the younger son the drums, and his three daughters the piano, accordion and xylophone, respectively. The ensemble was led by the violinist Maron Ashqar, who also arranged much of the repertoire the ensemble performed on many occasions at their concerts and broadcasts.

After the foundation of *Beit Ha–Gefen* as an Arab/Jewish Center in Haifa in 1965, Hikmat Shaheen who had previously been active in Tarshīha directed the musical activities at the Center. This soon developed into a music school, attracting many young men not only in Haifa but also from the surrounding area. Some years later it was possible to form an orchestra from those past students who had reached an advanced stage of proficiency. Many wellknown singers performed with this orchestra in activities organised by *Beit Ha–Gefen*. Several of the musicians involved in these developments later want abroad with considerable success.[1]

In 1963 the Ministry of Education made an enlightened decision in creating a Department of Arab Music within the Rubin Academy of Music in Haifa. I was fortunate enough to be appointed its first Director (this allowed me to be concerned with many of the major developments that took place in the following 20 years). Students came from all over Israel to follow the 2 year course that led to a special certificate in practical and theoretical studies. This course required attendance for two days a week and enabled graduates to work as qualified music teachers. More than 70 students graduated before the course was obliged to end through lack of funds in 1972.

Many graduates from this innovative department, considered to be amongst the finest musicians in Israel, were appointed music teachers. The first graduates from the Triangle[2] area – from Ṭaibe, Ṭira, 'Ara, and Kufur Qari', made a very great

---

[1] Nabil Azzam left for America in 1982 after completing his studies at the Tel-Aviv Music Academy. Following further study at the Hebrew University and the University of California he obtained his Ph.D. for his work on the Egyptian musician Abdul Wahāb.

Simon Shaheen Hikmat Shaheen's son, began performing on 'ūd and violin when he was still quite young; after studying at Tel-Aviv left Israel in the mid-1970s to perform throughout the USA with other excellent players from the Arab world.

Ibrahim Azzam, a talented singer in Hikmat Shaheen's group, went to London to work as a professional singer within the Arab community.

[2] The Triangle: a small area in the centre of Israel.

impact on the musical life of their villages where until then there had been no musical activity at all.

In 1966 an orchestra was established by the Haifa Conservatory students in the *Histradrut* center, *Beit Frank Sinatra*. This orchestra, which I led, had 15 players and gave special concerts until 1970, mainly in Nazareth.

The Renaissance of the 70s

A great many musical activities flourished throughout the country, including within the Triangle area. Dozens of ensembles were formed and performances took place in schools, clubs, and cultural and community centers. Programmes of music on radio and television were extremely successful and as a result new programmes were initiated.

At the time I was appointed music supervisor for Arab Schools, music in education developed considerably. Over 50 teachers were employed in some 130 schools. Many of them were able to form school choirs and, in order to help them in their work, song books were published, and courses and special meetings were held from time to time. 20 or more of these choirs took part in the annual festivals sponsored by the Ministry of Education in Haifa, Nazareth, Natania, Khidaira, and other centers.

The personnel of the Radio Orchestra was increased to 15 players and included two Arab violinists from Nazareth. Arab singers were employed to sing on radio programmes and many Arab singers and composers participated in the annual festivals held by the radio authorities in the big cities, Jerusalem, Tel-Aviv and Haifa. Two Jewish Egyptian musicians, Zuzu Mousa, who directed all these radio activities after 1971, and Zaki Srur, who was responsible for improving the programmes by introducing more than 100 songs, mostly of the prestigious genre *Muwashshaḥāt*, were important figures in these developments. Other festivals were held at *Beit Ha-more* (Teachers House) in Tel-Aviv and in Ramat Gan. They were directed by Izhak Avi-Ezer, a Jewish Iraqi scholar who introduced many groups and artists from the Arab communities including those from East Jerusalem.

Salim and Amal Shawqi, who had immigrated from Lebanon, added another style with their duet singing. They were also active in giving music lessons at the Conservatory in Jaffa and these attracted young Arabs from the south Triangle wanting singing and instrumental tuition.

In 1974 I was invited by the Director of the Arab section of the TV station to produce a music programme. We produced a folklore show which ran for two years with various *Zajal* singers. This was followed by a new programme, *Min Layālína*, for which a new orchestra, directed by Ṣudki Shukri, was created to accompany the popular singers from the Arab community. At first traditional songs were introduced and sung by Moshe Eliahu, a Jewish Syrian and Khalil Murani from Nazareth, who was popular in the radio programme *The Ship of Nūḥ* in which he sang, accompanied by Maron Ashqar playing the violin.

Three years later another programme was devised for TV called *Min Aghānīnā*. This programme which aimed at encouraging local composers and singers was successful in broadcasting more than 50 songs. In 1980 another programme went out under the title *Muwashshaḥāt*, with the cooperation of Zaki Srur and the radio orchestra and choir.

1974–1983 can be considered the golden era for the performance of Arab music on TV. Sadly, due to lack of funding these music programmes have ceased and since then few music programmes have been produced.

The 1980s

Musical activities continued to take place in most of the community centers and clubs. Many centers started music courses at which hundreds of youngsters began to learn and play different instruments. In the community center in Tamra an annual festival was started in 1977 and continues to the present day. Here dozens of artists – singers, and performers on various instruments – perform on stage. For the past three years there has been a composition competition as well.

A conservatory was opened in Nazareth where many pupils are still studying instrumental skills on ʿūd, violin (both Oriental and European techniques), piano, organ, and guitar. Another conservatoire was opened in Tarshīḥa, but is no longer active because of a lack of students. There were two other attempts to start conservatories; these failed because the Ministry of Education considered the teachers unqualified and the curriculum unacceptable.

In 1981 and 1984 I directed two new music classes in the Arab Teacher Training College in Haifa. Some 30 or more students attended the three year courses that included Arab and European music. The graduates from both classes have been appointed as qualified music teachers in a number of Arab schools.

During this decade a great many Wedding ensembles were formed and most artists found that performance at these events was more profitable than any other work. Some teachers joined these ensembles to provide a second source of income.

The Early 1990s

In the late 80s the choir *Bath* was founded in Shefaamr, directed by Rahib Ḥaddād, a graduate from the piano class at the Rubin Academy in Haifa. At the beginning there were about 20 members. They sang Arab songs, mostly Lebanese, accompanied by the organ. As the years went by more and more people joined the choir and the repertoire was broadened to include songs arranged by Raḥbānī musicians from Lebanon, some *Muwashshaḥāt* and national songs. The choir gave concerts last year in the Haifa Auditorium and in Nazareth and Bīr Zeit as well as taking part in the festival in Acre.

Another choir, composed entirely of inhabitants of Tarshīḥa, was founded in 1990, directed by the violinist Nasim Dakwar. The choir was joined by 10/12 players for their concerts. The repertoire of the choir and ensemble is mainly *Muwashshaḥāt* and traditional Egyptian songs. They had successful concerts in the Haifa Auditorium and in November gave a concert in the Opera House in Cairo, under the name *Palestine* as the Opera House administration refused to allow them to appear as representatives of Israel.

A small group of Arab and Jewish musicians founded the *Bustān Ensemble*, led by Taisīr Elias, from Shafaamr. He had studied at the Hebrew University in Jerusalem and is now considered one of the finest players of ʿūd and violin. Their repertoire is a mixture of Arab and European music. For the last two years they have performed all over Israel as well as touring abroad.

The Arab Music Orchestra

The Arab Music Orchestra

The Arab Music orchestra was founded in 1990 by the Arab Cultural Department and receives financial support from the Ministry of Science and Art. Since November 1991 the orchestra has worked under the sponsorship of the Rubin Academy of Music in Haifa. The orchestra, which I was invited to direct, consists of 21 players (Arabs and Jews). There are 8 violins, 2 violas, 3 'cellos, 1 double bass, 3 'ūds, qanum, nāy, and 2 drums (darbukka and tambourine).

The orchestra plays Classical Arab music and selections from the compositions of the great composers of the Arab world.[3] In the last two years special emphasis has been given to compositions by local composers in order to encourage the musical creatively of Israeli composers.[4] A selection of these compositions, vocal and instrumental, were performed at a Gala Concert in Nazareth in April 1994,

---

[3]   Abdul Wahāb (d. 1991) Egyptian, Farīd Aṭrash (d. 1974) Egyptian, Muḥammad Qasabji (d. 1966) Egyptian, Tatyus, a Turkish 19th century composer.

[4]   Nicar Radwan, Michael Dermelkonian.

and repeated later in the month in Haifa. The texts of most of the songs highlighted the theme of peace and Arab/Jewish coexistence.

The orchestra performs to audiences of Arabs and Jews, adults and youth, in towns, villages, and *kibbutzim* celebrating various occasions throughout the whole country. In the past year the orchestra has given over 25 concerts to more than 10,000 people, and received the 'Cylinder' Prize of the department of Ommanut La'am. In 1995 the orchestra is planning to give 4 concerts in Haifa, 4 subscription concerts in Nazareth, and take part in the special festival in June with the cooperation of *Beit Ha-gefen* in Haifa.

The Arab Music Orchestra playing at a public concert.

New Music Centers

The Center for the Absorbtion of Immigrant Artists, a joint organisation of the Ministry of Absorbtion, the Ministry of Education and the Jewish Agency, has initiated and is currently establishing music centers to serve special population segments of Israeli society. The core purpose of this effort is to find work for immigrant musicians and utilise their skills to contribute in the field of education and culture, within a framework that will integrate the specific needs of the Arab and Druze population. Ten centers have been established in the last two years, including those in Baqa al-Garbiya, Saknin, Majd-al Kurūm, Nazareth, Beit Jān, Abu Snān, and 'Usufiya. In all these centers the emphasis has been placed on

European music, played on the piano, organ, violin, guitar, and other Western instruments: little interest has been given to authentic Arab music.

* * *

In summarizing the situation in regard to the performance of Arab music in Israel at the present time one must first draw attention to the fact that hundreds of young people are playing music on many occasions and for many purposes. Though singers participate on these occasions all over the country it is unfortunate that the kind of music played and sung mainly consists of cheap songs performed in a pop-rock style, imitating the Anglo-American rhythmic patterns, using keyboard instruments, bass guitar, and with an emphasis on the rhythmic role played by the drums, cymbal, and tambourine.

Traditional instruments are losing their importance in these ensembles.

The main goal of the singers and players is to motivate the young people to dance in a hysterical way. The songs are performed in a monotonous style that tries to imitate the popular singers of Egypt and Lebanon. On the other hand there are a few ensembles, including the Arab Music Orchestra, that attracts a special kind of audience that appreciates the authentic and traditional music played at concerts given in concert halls.

In a few villages folklore singers are still performing at social events and marriage parties, singing various forms of *Ḥidā, Mejana, ʿAtāba,* and *Mḥorabe.* These folk songs are usually sung without instrumental accompaniment. However, in the past two years more than 20 dance groups have been formed in different village centers using *Shubbāba, Urghūl* and *Darbukka* for accompaniment.

Music by Arab Composers

The first two pieces are by young Arab composers, encouraged by the Arab Music Orchestra.

1. *Samāʿi Hijāz Kār* (1994) is by Nizar Radwan. *Samāʿi* is a Turkish form similar to the Rondo. Every *Samāʿi* is divided into 4 *Khanes* (parts). After each part of section the initial *taslīm* (refrain) is repeated. This work is based on the maqām *Hijāz Kār.*

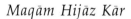

Maqām Hijāz Kār

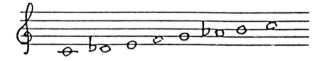

b indicates a quarter tone

2. *Fikra* is a free composition by Michael Dermelkonian.

SAMĀʿĪ HĪJĀZ KĀR

Nizar Radwan

FIKRA

Michael Dermalkonian

These next three pieces are compositions by composers of earlier generations.

3. *Zikrayāti* (My memories) by Muḥammad Qasabji

4. *Samāʻi Huzām* by Abdul Wahāb, considered the finest composer in the Arab world, died in 1991.

5. *Samāʻi Rast* by Tatyus

Huzām and *Rast* are *maqām* (modes). *Maqām Rast* starts with a tetrachord of one whole tone followed by two 3/4 tones.

   A CD on which these 5 pieces can be heard, performed by the Arab Music Orchestra will be provided with Part II.

ZIKRAYĀTI
Qasabji

SAMĀ'Ī HUZĀM
Abdul-Wahab

سماعي هزام لعبدالوهاب

SAMĀ'Ī RAST

Tatyus

Musical Performance,
1997, Vol. 1, Part 2, pp. 51–63
Reprints available directly from the publisher
Photocopying permitted by license only

Ashkenazi Liturgical Music in Israel Today

A Short Social History and Review

Raymond Goldstein

The re-awakening of the Ashenazi tradition in Israel. The golden age of recorded hazzanut and the present day cantor's reactions. Establishment of cantorial academies. A short social European history of Ashkenazi liturgical music. The medium of concerts. The restrictions on the orthodox cantor. The creation of a new concert repertoire. The advent of the phonograph record and its influence. Virtuoso recitatives and the use of extemporised *nusah*. The different viewpoint of the Orthodox tradition. The hiring of guest cantors for important shabbat and festival occasions. Financial considerations. Popular taste in liturgical music appreciation. The aspect of the choir in the synagogue; signs of Israel's liturgical music revival. The broadcast of religious music on state radio; TV, Cassettes and CDs. *Renanot*, The Institute of Sacred Music. Sheet music. Jacob Michael collection of Jewish music. Prospects for cantors at home and abroad.

KEY WORDS and PHRASES *Golden Age Cantors*, Ashkenazi Liturgical Music, *Nusaḥ*, Renanot, Synagogue, Jacob Michel Collection of Jewish Music.

Over the last few years, there has been a new re-awakening on the part of the public as to the revival of the Jewish cantorial art known as *hazzanut* or *hazonis* as typified by the Ashkenazi tradition, both in Israel and the diaspora. Whenever a concert is advertised at an important venue such as Tel Aviv's Mann Auditorium the organizers can usually be assured of a packed house, or at least a favorable attendance, if some of the cantors performing are among the present day stars. These stars, both in concert and in the pulpit, have since the advent of the mass media – radio, TV and concert hall – encouraged and promoted the art. Thus it is not uncommon on a Tuesday night, when Kol Yisrael (The Israel Broadcasting Authority) has its weekly cantorial concert, for its public to include the secular and religious. The love of *hazzanut* doesn't demand that you have to be religious or even *Ashkenazi*, it is just a feeling of belonging and sentiment found in all people who adore soul music with its *steigerim* (scales), *nusahot* (melodic patterns or prayers modes), inherent harmonies and everpresent virtuosity. Jewish spiritual music not only consists of *hazzanut*, but includes *hasidic* music and the art of the *klezmer*. All three strata find themselves not only the subject of concerts but of festivals as well (e.g. the *Klezmer* festival of Safad). The word *Klezmer*[1] is a Yiddish term meaning instrument, it is also used to describe the iterrerant musicians who fulfilled the artistic and cultural needs of the Jewish community.

Though *Klezmer* and authentic *hasidic* music are important subjects on their own, we refer to them only in the context of their liturgical usuage.

---

[1]   From the Hebrew *Kley-zemer* – instrument of song.

The golden age[2] when the great *hazzanut* recorded was in the first half of this century. Since the death of such famous cantors as Rosenblatt (see figure l) Kwartin, Sirota, and in the subsequent generation the Kousseviskys, Pinchik and others,[3] many of our present day cantors have kept up this popular tradition by performing this same repertoire, both in concert and synagogue. However, in Israel, not everyone in this profession has the ability to read music; the performance of recitatives has often had to depend on the cantor's musicianship and vocal prowess (or lack of it!). Steps to improve this situation in Israel are not something new. We can note that since the beginning of the century various cantorial academies have existed, as seen in the work of Abraham Zvi Idelsohn (1882–1938), Zalman Rivlin of Jerusalem and Leibele Glantz (1898–1964). However, since the death or emigration of these men, their schools have ceased to exist. At best the training was on an informal, subjective basis, particularly in the case of the Jerusalem teacher/conductor Rivlin.

For his time Rivlin probably had the right approach to the subject; all his pupils sang in his famous choir and so with this practical experience of participation they were able to continue to this day using his *nusah* and melodies wherever they act as cantors or *ba'ale-tefilah* (leader of the services – lay cantors.) Among his famous students were Yehoshua Lerer and the composer Tzvi Talmon. To this day we speak of *Nusah Yerushalmi* (Jerusalem) when referring to the repertoire of his students. It is fortunate that 2 volumes of *nusahot* were published preserving this tradition. The same can be said for both Idelsohn and Leibele Glantz. Another important teacher with a similar approach to choir participation was to be found in Tel Aviv – Schlomo Ravitz at the Bilu synagogue. This centenarian passed away a decade ago but he has left us a legacy in a 2 volume anthology called *Kol Yisrael*

---

[2]   The *Golden Age Cantors* is a general term often used by those writing about *hazzanut* recordings of the 20s and 30s. It was never used by the Cantors themselves. Most of the best and more famous Cantors, who were prepared to record, usually did so for RCA Victor (USA) or HMV (UK), or Columbia, on both sides of the Atlantic. The royalties were often quite substantial.

[3]   Rosenblatt himself made over 200 recordings. In the era of the LP one company re-issued around 17 volumes of his material.

During the 20s and 30s a great number of 78s were sold and distributed throughout the world; most of them were re-issued on LP in the 50s and 60s, and a few have now become available on CD. Several Israeli companies have re-issued cassettes to satisfy the demand, usually from their religious customers, for the older recordings. In addition recordings made by a later generation of Cantors (the Koussevitsky Brothers and others) have been issued. The Collector's Guild and the Greater Record Company (GRC) are famous for their re-issue of the older 78 recordings, and two other companies, Banner and Tikva Records have also issued many Cantorial recordings.

At first most recordings were made with harmonium or organ accompaniment because they recorded reasonably well. Later piano and chamber ensemble arrangements were provided by amongst others Saslavsky Rumshinsky; flute, clarinet, french horn, and string quartet, sometimes with the addition of piano, was a popular backing. It was only on the later recordings by Moshe Koussevitsky, Richard Tucker, and Jan Pearce that full orchestral arrangements by Warner Bass, Shalom Secunda, and Abe Ellstein were commissioned, probably by the record company. More recently Cantors have often chosen and commissioned arrangements themselves, usually because they identify with a particular arranger. By this time the settings had been thoroughly worked out, in contrast to the earlier recordings when they will have been extemporized in the course of the recording.

When the sheet music of the various recitatives was published it frequently varied in detail from the recording, whether the music was published before or after the recording. The recorded performance probably depended as much on the condition of the Cantor's voice on that occasion as the inspiration of the moment.

Figure 1 Moshe Koussevitsky

– (the voice of Israel) edited by Geshuri. In Haifa Yitchak Heilman, though an octogenarian, continues a similar tradition. His music still awaits publication.

Today in the 1990's though there is certainly no shortage of private teachers, there is no recognized, accredited university diploma or degree for professional cantors. In the USA both the reform (HUC) and the conservative movement (JTS) and the orthodox *Yeshiva* university has rectified this situation. It is often difficult for a cantor without going through one of these programmes to get himself a permanent job in an affiliated temple or synagogue. In Israel various universities do offer courses in Jewish music – but often with an emphasis on the *Sephardi* style and tradition at the expense of a deeper understanding of Israeli *Ashkenazi nusah.* Perhaps this is owing to neglect of the *Sephardi* tradition over previous years.

Hazzanut as a subject for teaching has found quite a number of private teachers who have opened up their own schools teaching usually on a one to one basis. An exception to this often haphazard approach can be found in the Tel Aviv Cantorial Institute which has been supported for the last couple of years by the Tel Aviv Municipality thanks in no small way to former Lord Mayor Schlomo Lahat. The students are given both group and individual classes and an emphasis is put on allied music subjects such as solfege and general music appreciation. Guest lecturers are invited and the school boasts a good library of scores and recordings. Here, one of the main aims is to give the student a varied approach to the study of *nusah* so that in the course of a number of years he will have learned different approaches to the subject.

Certain social factors in Israeli religious society have not exactly made the professional role of the cantor easy. Though everyone may enjoy *hazzanut*, the question is where, how, and for whom it should be performed. Ironically the problem today for many orthodox Jews is whether *hazzanut* should be kept for the pulpit or allowed as a secular/religious experience in concert halls. If we review the events and influences of the past we shall see how this has arisen.

Over the years the position of cantor or precentor, whose duty it is to lead the congregation in prayer, has evolved from that of layman to that of a fully fledged professional. With the establishment of our *nushaot* (prayer tunes), the rise of opera, and the indirect influence of the church, the congregation gradually demanded more of music in their approach to prayer in the synagogue.

Since time immemorial the cantor has always had to have a pleasant voice and pleasing disposition, knowledge of *perush hamila* (real understanding of the word) and an innate ability to lead his congregation in prayer and praise. Until the 19th century, the *Ashkenazi* cantor was often accompanied by his *singeral* (generally a boy soprano – more often than not his son) and a bass (usually an adult with a lower voice than that of the cantor). More often than not the congregation would be more interested in tenors (and high baritones) than basses. As in opera tenors with their high tessitura, tend to create an elevated feeling of excitement (religious fervour) in their congregations. Indeed as research by Eduard Birnbaum (1855–1920) and later by the Jewish music research centre (Hebrew University) has shown, 18th century liturgy owes a good deal to 'borrowings' from famous Italian opera arias, often with scant regard to the scansion of the Hebrew language. *Ashkenazi* Hebrew pronunciation had always been more lenient on this subject than the modern *Sephardi* usuage in most of present day Israeli *Ashkenazi* synagogues. Hebrew is a living, day to day language in Israel and not just *sefet kodesh* (the holy language), the average man in the street is far more aware of the correct stresses of the language than ever before. In the 18th century very little original synagogal music existed and the ancient melodies quoted as being from Mount Sinai were usually passed down by rote.

It is not the purpose of this essay to deal with the beginnings of Jewish liturgical music in the synagogue, as opposed to that of the ancient Temple, or even to the influence of the Christian church until the renaissance. Nevertheless we should be aware of the influence of the emancipation and the *emfinsamkeit* movement in addition to the role of the Lutheran church with its all encompassing powerful chorale singing in 4 parts by both congregation and choir alike. Luther introduced the chorale as a way of creating unity among his worshippers, and thus it was only a matter of time before Jewish reformers like the famous 19th century cantor – composer Salamon Sulzer (1804–1890) introduced 4 part singing into the synagogue. After studying music in Switzerland and Germany, he became cantor in his home town of Hohenems where he remained until 1825. In 1826 he accepted the post of Oberkantor at Vienna's famous Seitenstettengasse Temple, a post he held for forty five years and where he not only rejuvenated synagogue song but proved to be the main influence on European synagogue music. Unlike the cantors before him, when it came to singing compositions, Sulzer would always make sure that the music was notated and worked out in the classical manner of the time. He required help with this mammoth task and so he enlisted the help of Christian church composers to write original music for his synagogue (e.g. Fishoff, von Seyfried and even Schubert).

Pleasant though their compositions are one could certainly not call them masterpieces and *nusaḥ* certainly didn't seem to be of much concern. Nevertheless this was all an improvement on what had been the former situation where music had been haphazardly performed in a rather primitive fashion in the extemporised style of the cantor, singeral and bass who would harmonize in simple 3rds and 6ths with a rudimentary pedal point.

From the Sulzer school many fine composers developed the *Ashkenazi* choral tradition into the force it is today – Lewandowsky in Berlin; Naumbourg in Paris; Dunajewesky and Nowakowsky in Russia, the latter also influenced by the Russian orthodox church traditions. From Lewandowsky, we have the Handel–Mendelssohn tradition of heroic oratorio-styled choruses sweeping the congregation off its feet. His counterpoint proved to be the best of all the 19th century composers, so much so that his SATB compositions are easily adaptable for TTBB choirs as found in Israel to this day (see Music Example 1). Besides writing for the liturgical year all the above also wrote works for state occasions sometimes even with organ (and harp) accompaniment. However, as a rule the playing of instruments as background or accompaniment on the shabbath and holidays was frowned upon, as their prohibition was a sign of respect for the destruction of the 2nd temple. At any rate it was only in the liberal synagogues that it was accepted. To this day, some Rabbis in Israel still frown on the use of an organ in a service even on a weekday, though the synagogue remains a popular venue for a *ḥazzanut* concert.

An increased knowledge of music notation, the influence of good singing, heard in local opera houses, and easier travelling facilities brought about an even greater cross exchange of ideas. As a result cantors developed the ability to dazzle their congregants with their coloratura, range, and often exquisite use of falsetto. The more musical cantors found that they were creating new and original works that

Music Example 1   Ps. 150. "Hallelujah" by Louls Lewandowski starts with the following English text.

"Hallelujah! Proclaim God through the praise of his mighty acts in His Sanctuary; proclaim Him in the firmament of His invincible power."

would be suitable vehicles for their particular voices and techniques. This approach would reach its climax in the golden age of cantors who through the gramophone would promote the cantorial art beyond their wildest dreams.

In Eastern Europe until the holocaust any decent synagogue wishing to engage a fine cantor always tried to promise an accompanying choir so that the cantor and choir could then be part of the *gesamtkunstwerk* of the service. With such a result at hand, many fine compositions came into being. It should be remembered that the Jew in Eastern Europe often used the synagogue as his opera house and concert hall; sometimes, due to social conditions, the synagogue was often the only place where a Jew could in the same place pray, relax, and enjoy a service. Thus inordinately long services lasting several hours often became commonplace on a Sabbath or Festival morning with the congregant being given a feast of musical fare that would wet his appetite for more on the next occasion. In Israel today, as there is no Sunday, and Saturday is the only day of rest, people don't really have the patience for this phenomena though one should point to legendary cantor Moishe Stern who still packs the 'houses' with this type of lengthy service. As a guest cantor, doing festive shabbath services it is fine, but like rich fruitcake it should only be indulged in occasionally.

As a result, and with an ever increasing interest in this art, cantors who were often on tour, saw the medium of concerts as yet another worthwhile enterprise. For the orthodox cantor the restrictions in Israel were far fewer. Here at least he could be accompanied by either piano (Harmonium), choir and/or orchestra, the latter a far more recent occurrence in Israel, due to public demand. He was thus able to entertain those who couldn't attend his synagogue services (often for practical and/or religious reasons). From the concert has developed the special repertoire that may not have been thought of for musical performance in the actual synagogue service, or perhaps is of a different liturgical text, such as an extract from the Psalms, Song of Songs, and other extracts from the bible and/or religious poetical texts (*piyyut*). Sometimes it consisted of material not necessarily in the tradition of the synagogue – but certainly viable as religious literature. (e.g. *Ashkenazi* renditions of texts like *Raza de shabbat* which do not appear in the *Ashkenazi siddur*, as sung in versions by Pinchik and Mandelbaum).

Ironically, it has often happened that repertoire first heard at these cantorial concerts has somehow made its way into the synagogue, as opposed to the other way round. Some settings, like Rosenblatt's *Ad Hena*, normally not said by the Oberkantor as it appears too early in the sabbath morning service. Rosenblatt was famous for taking a text not normally sung, and making a composition of it, as in *Ve-af Hu*, which is part of the penitential prayers of *Yom Kippur* (The Day of Atonement) (see Figure 2).

Another influence that soon made its presence felt was the advent of the phonograph record at the beginning of the 20th century. Ironically, at first for religious reasons, quite a number of cantors refused to record. In Israel recording started relatively late, during the British mandate days, and it was only with the advent of the LP that companies like Hed Arzi started in earnest to record the popular cantors of the day Yitchak Eshel, Yehoshua Lerer, Benjamin Ungar. These were some of the leading cantors in some of the largest synagogues of the time. Often the local record companies would invite visiting cantors to cut a few discs while on tour in Israel (e.g. David Kusevitsky[4] and the Malavsky family), but in the main the records of the Golden age cantors were re-released under licence by the local companies or else imported from abroad.[5]

It should be remembered that with the beginning of electrical recording in the mid '20s the Golden age cantors became the superstars of their time – most of them recorded for HMV, Columbia and RCA Victor ... (Kwartin, Chagy, Hershman, Pinchik, the Koussevitsky Brothers and, of course, the most inventive of them all – Yosselle Rosenblatt – who ironically died here in the Holy Land while making a movie (and escaping his creditors). Rosenblatt made a particularly strong impression on the religious public in Israel in the '30s. His funeral in Jerusalem was one of the largest ever held there.

The LP appeared at the end of the '40s. The cognensci immediately snapped up whatever compilations of the Golden Age cantors the recording companies issued.[5] As a result the new generation of cantors were no longer asked by their public to sing specific compositions but '. . . .' as sung by cantor X. It is interesting to note that not all Golden age cantors were composers; some were primarily performers of recitatives composed by other less vocally gifted cantors, such as Hershman, who specialized in the extemporisations compositions of Rappaport – a well known American cantor of his time.

This would all be very well, were it not for the sad fact that many of the present performers do not have the necessary vocal and/or musical ability, nor even the basic facial bone structure that gave certain cantors a unique sound, as in the case of the Koussevitsky Brothers.[4] Still, the average listener doesn't really care, as can be judged from their reactions in today's concert halls. Many of these recorded recitatives which were sung to show off the virtuosity of their performers have now, together with the use of extemporised *nusaḥ* and bona fide compositions become the mainstay of the modern synagogue service. Curiously enough, apart from a handful of publications eminating from the USA many of these great recitatives remain out of print so one must be thankful to master transcribers, like New York's Noah Schall and Israel's own Schmuel Baruch Taube, for their painstaking work in transcribing 1000's of these famous recorded recitatives so that everyone may be able to learn and study these works with the music in front of them instead of being obliged to learn them by rote.

Other factors that indicate an approach to a given service are the geographical position, denomination and tradition of a given congregation in Israel today, the state religion is the Orthodox movement. Conservative and Reform tradition synagogues are to be found in every large city, but they are relatively few in number, and while they incorporate Israeli *nusaḥot* and customs in their services they are still largely influenced by their liberal German or American reform parents and are beyond the scope of this essay.

---

[4]   The transliteration of the Russian Cyrillic script and Hebrew characters has led to a considerable variation in the spelling of Cantors' names. In the case of the Koussevitsky Brothers, one of the brothers, Moshe, is always spelt Koussevitsky, whilst his brothers Simca, David and Jacob are Kusevitsky. When they are written about collectively one may find either used.

[5]   Yosselle (Joseph) Rosenblatt 1882–1933; Zevulun Kwartin 1874–1952; Mordechai Hershman 1888–1940; Moshe Koussevitsky 1899–1966; Jacob Kusevitsky 1903–1959; Simca Kusevitsky 1905– still living in South Africa; David Kusevitsky 1911–1985; Pierre Pinchik; David Roitman 1884–1943; Berele Chagy 1892–1954; Yitchak Eshel 1915–; Yehoshua Lerer pre-1930–; Benjamin Ungar 1907–1982 (?); Jacob Rappaport 1890–1943.

Figure 2 Two representatives of bel canto. The meeting of Josef (Yossele) Rosenblatt and Tito Scipa, March, 1925.

Our Orthodox tradition is split into various levels; each approaches the aspect of synagogue music from a different viewpoint. The ultra-orthodox (the *Haredim*) though true lovers of the cantorial art tend to leave *hazzanut* more for the concert hall, and concentrate more on the *devekut* (holy deepness) of prayer itself. They feel that *hazzanut* with its pyrotechnics can too often be at the expense of the *tefillah* (prayer) itself. Another restriction is that the repetition of words is usually frowned upon though repetition is one of the pillars of many cantorial recitatives; nevertheless their *nusah* is often filled with beautiful *Hasidic* chant and each *Hasidic* sect has its own set of melodies with which to enrich the service.

Congregational participation is greatly encouraged and it certainly leaves no place for formal choral singing. The presenter is usually a *shaliyah tzibbur* (representative of the congregation) and though it helps if he has a pleasing voice it is not essential. Despite this somewhat casual approach to *hazzanut* in the synagogue many of Israel's finer cantors today are from the *Haredi* and *Yeshiva* world.

Hiring a guest cantor for an important shabbat and/or festival is nevertheless still popular in all the big synagogues, be they Haredi or Modern Orthodox. In the end it is a question of finance: the better the cantor, the higher his fee is likely to be. Israel has many more *stibels* (small synagogues) than big main sanctuaries; it will often be a financial problem for many of the smaller congregations to engage a cantor, let alone set up a choir. Recently, aspiring cantors, whether graduates of cantorial academies or not, complain of an explosion of candidates looking for the chance to make some extra income, particularly during the high Holiday season. This has brought down the fee offered by many congregations. Most of these cantors are modern orthodox and for reasons of deep personal faith are usually not keen to undertake jobs in conservative or reform congregations abroad despite the higher remuneration that is offered.

Nonetheless quite a number do travel abroad each year in search of that pot of gold at the end of the rainbow. Fewer and fewer orthodox congregations abroad are now hiring cantors for the holidays due to budget cuts, depression, etc. Because of the competition some agents, particularly in the USA, are exploiting the situation.

Hasidic music is very popular in Israel but apart from a few professionals it is all too often a pale imitation of the real thing. Unfortunately commercialism has played a part in not giving the public the opportunity of hearing the real thing. It should be born in mind that the public for *Hasidic* music is not very sophisticated. They approach this music as they might regular secular pop music.

Among many congregations this has almost been the death sentence for *hazzanut*. Many cantors, wishing to make themselves popular with their congregations, introduce melodies that are often not the appropriate *nusah* for a particular text. Among the worst offenders are the 'Young Israel' movement, who are also guilty of stylising our beautiful free *nusahot* and too often develop fixed melodic patterns which they repeat like parrots from one service to the next without leaving room for any extemporisation. It has now arrived at the point when certain texts for some festivals/sabbaths have to be sung to a number of set tunes which have become resistant to change. These are the only ones their fellow congregants know. 'Young Israel' do encourage community singing, but at what a price. Perhaps this author is being too severe – but surely every sensitive religious musician would find it impossible to listen to the same mundane *Bnei 'Akiva* tunes over and over again, week after week.

At least in the bigger modern Orthodox synagogues, this problem is less pronounced. The Jerusalem Great Synagogue (which is a rare example of the *chorshuel* (lit. a choir synagogue in the old tradition), has the only professional adult male choir that performs practically weekly with only a few shabbaths off in the year, but there are various other large synagogues in the big cities that have a choir at least once if not twice a month besides Holidays. The JGS takes pride in not only having a fine cantor (Naphtali Herstik), but also engages a professional symphonic conductor (Elli Jaffe) as well as a music arranger (Raymond Goldstein) to keep up a new and fresh approach to liturgical music in Israel. The repertoire is constantly being updated, amended and added to and as a result it is one of the leading lights in the Israeli world of liturgy. New compositions and approaches are constantly being sought so that the musical part of the service is of interest to all. Certainly there are universal melodies that the whole Jewish world loves – these are of course kept as the standard repertoire, but there is an emphasis on variety whenever possible. Though services are generally somewhat longer than in the smaller establishments attention is always paid to the length of the service thereby preventing boredom or even frustration on the part of the congregation (see Music Example 2).

In keeping within the confines of strict orthodox practice, all choirs are male and the singing is a capella. Today unfortunately the synagogue choirs have only adults. The heyday of boy choirs in the synagogue are over for various reasons. Few conductors today have the patience to deal with the boisterous behaviour of Israeli youth and the general lack of discipline. One needs to be a disciplinarian as well as a musician to handle such a group. Though Israel is an exceptionally musical country in all other respects, its youth more often than not has never been exposed to a strong classical music tradition and few know how to read music let alone have any choral tradition at their fingertips. Thus teaching choral parts has to be done by rote.

In conclusion, let me state that despite the current low state of liturgical music making in the diaspora, often for financial reasons, it is at present showing signs of revival. There are several reasons for this:

(i)   An increase in the number of cantorial concerts in the major cities, thanks to the efforts of the various departments of torah culture; commercial ventures by private impressarios, and the use of the cantorial concert as a means of raising money for charity. Though we have excellent world class cantors, there is still some unfortunate snobbism at the thought of imported cantors, which might improve the box office.

This is all quite ironic as many of them are *yordim* – Israelis who now reside permanently outside Israel. Another important point that should not be overlooked is the higher standard of accompaniment available to cantors now that more and more proper concert arrangements are becoming available for the main concert repertoire.

(ii) The establishment of the Tel Aviv Cantorial Institute and other smaller schools and an increase in the number of individual cantors teaching the profession. Criticism is sometimes levelled at those who insist on teaching only their own *nusaḥ* as opposed to giving their pupils more knowledge and understanding of the repertoire of the last 150 years.

(iii) The broadcasting of religious music on state radio and TV. The programmes often consist of live and prerecorded concerts performed throughout the country. The better concerts are kept in the radio's archives and, by public demand, are repeated from time to time through the years.

(iv) Too often the easy availability of cassettes and CDs of the "Golden Age of Ḥazzanut" has led the younger generation to copy their predecessors in repertoire and style. With regard to the study of *nusaḥ. Renanot*, the Institute of Sacred Music, headed by the indefatigable Ezra Barnea has put out various sets of *nusaḥ.* (on cassette) covering not only the *Ashkenazi* tradition, but the various *Sephardi* ones as well. The cassettes cover, Shabbat, Festivals (the 3 Regalim, Pilgrim Festivals of Passover, Pentecost and tabernacles) and the High Holidays.

Music Example 2   I. Gottbetter's: *Lo Amut* (I shall not die) is taken from the *Halle* ("praise") service performed on most festivals. The text is from Psalm of David (Ps:118) "I shall not die! But I shall live and relate the deeds of the Lord. The Lord has chastised me heavily, but He has not given me over to death."

Gottbetter was for many years choirmaster at a synagogue in Rostov on Don. This excellent example of his work is one of the few to have been prepared via a notation programme. It is for Cantor and 4 part a cappella choir (TTBB), with a *bocca chiosa* accompaniment in lieu of organ. In memory of the destruction of the 2nd Temple the playing of all musical instruments is prohibited at synagogue services on the Sabbath and Festivals. Before the destruction instruments were regularly in use (see: Alfred Sendry, *Music in Ancient Israel*, Philosophical Library, New York, 1969).

(v) Sheet music: apart from the few publications supplied by *Renanot*, little is available in print. The Israeli publishers usually shy away from the religious establishment as they cater mainly for the secular society. Unfortunately Israeli congregations and their cantors have to order volumes of recitatives from the USA or else contact cantorial recitatives libraries which are in private hands.

The national library houses the famous Jacob Michael collection of Jewish music. The collection was acquired from the United States a few decades ago and must surely count as one of the most important of its kind. It is housed in the music department of the National and University Library. Because of the influence of concerts, radio and the cantorial schools, there has for a number of years been an every growing renaissance in the appreciation of good cantorial singing in our synagogues. In this connection it should be remembered that the position was very different only 40 years ago. People were a lot less materialistic then, and so many more synagogues possessed choirs and cantors. The European/American tradition was stronger in this connection because most of that generation had arrived in Israel just a few years before.

Full time cantorial appointments are few and far between and even those few who are lucky enough to obtain a position must turn to teaching or some other profession to supplement their income. Most of the well paid cantorial jobs exist in North America. However, many are no longer in the Orthodox movement for the reasons stated above.

Musical Performance,
1997, Vol. 1, Part 2, pp. 65–79
Reprints available directly from the publisher
Photocopying permitted by license only

Music and Cantillation in the Sephardi Synagogue

Ezra Barnea

This article notes that the Sephardi Synagogue songs that have been handed down from generation to generation for hundreds of years have recently gained momentum and absorbed various influences as a result of the ingathering of exiles to modern Israel.

It also draws attention to the role of the Cantors and the impact of the synagogue on the yearly cycle and the congregant's lives.

The impact of composers and artists active in this field is examined. Today the song-culture of the synagogue has left the confines of intimacy and now enters public life as a result of media exposure.

KEY WORDS   Sephardi Synagogue Song, The Cantor, Baqqashot, Maqām.

Cantillation in the Sephardi synagogue incorporates cantorial traditions that have been handed down from generation to generation for hundreds of years. In the wake of recent waves of immigration these traditions have been deeply influenced by the cultural impact of the different ethnic groups that have settled in Israel.

The Sephardi synagogue has always been characterized by communal singing which accompanies the service. Although there is usually no official synagogue choir, the whole congregation provides a choral accompaniment for the cantor, who leads the service and occupies the centre of the stage.

The cantor's task is to compose or improvise musical themes, or alternately to adapt well-known melodies (not necessarily Jewish in origin), to the liturgical texts. Once these themes have been incorporated into the service, they become part of an oral tradition that will be passed on to future generations.

As early as the 10th century C.E., liturgical singing was much enriched as a result of the flowering of Jewish culture in Spain, and particularly by Donash Ben-Lavrat, who immigrated from Baghdad to Cordova in the middle of the 10th century.[1] Donash, who was then an accomplished cantor, poet, and composer, adapted to Hebrew poetry the pattern of the classical Arabic quantitative metre which is essentially built on distinguishing clearly between the short and long syllables that comprise a word. Donash assigned the semivowel *sheva na'* (mobile sheva) to the short syllable, and all vocalized consonants to the long ones; he called his system *yetedot* (short units with a mobile sheva, combined with long vocalized consonants) and *tenu'ot* (long units comprising vocalized consonants).

Five hundred years later, in very different circumstances, Rabbi Israel Najjara did much the same as his predecessor. He composed most of his liturgical hymns according to the syllabic meter then used in Italy, but quite a few in accordance with the older classical Arabic tradition. It is known that Rabbi Najjara, a poet of

---

[1]   See Amnon Shiloah, Development of Jewish Liturgical Singing in Spain, *The Sephardi Legacy*, ed. Haim Beinart, Vol. II, Magnes Press, Jerusalem, 1992, 423–437.

eminent social standing, belonged to the intellectual aristocracy that favoured poetic writing in the old Spanish tradition. His hymns are still part of the liturgy and are often heard in the synagogue and on festive occasions.

From the 12th century onwards travellers who visited countries where there were isolated Jewish communities kept records that include their impressions of the synagogue services. Here are some examples of the earliest evidence relating to the cantor's role in the service.

In his book *Tahkemoni*,[2] Rabbi Yehudah Alharizi tells of his visit to Baghdad in 1120 C.E. He describes a cantor who attempted to lead a group of youths in song and prayer on the Sabbath. Alharizi is scathingly critical of the cantor, who made mistakes in the elementary reading of the service. Apparently, the congregants were so disenchanted by his performance, that they began to leave while he was still conducting the service. However, in spite of the severe criticism, the cantor was obviously a musician.[3]

From the account given by Rabbi Binyamin of Tudela and Rabbi Petahya of Regenzburg of their visit to Baghdad, it can be seen that communal singing was quite usual in the synagogue,[4] and it must be remembered that at that time the Jewish community of Baghdad was large and prosperous.

Another equally large Jewish centre attracted visitors, and here too we have the record kept by R. Yehuda Alharizi of his travels.[5] He writes: 'From there I came to the royal city, blessed Aram Sova'. He refers to Aleppo, in Syria, and here his impression was quite different from what he reported from his visit to Baghdad. After a detailed description of the leaders and sages in Aleppo he goes on to describe the cantor: '. . . of them the Rabbi Daniel, whose singing is tuneful and who conducts the service well. His singing conquers the hearts of the holy congregation, and his voice will surely be heard as he approaches the Trisagion.[6]

The Role of the Cantor

The cantor should have not only a pleasing voice, but also musicality, which may be natural or acquired.

Apart from liturgical music, the cantor's repertoire should include songs for festive occasions, such as the birth of a son or a daughter, the redemption of a first-born son, a Bar-Mitzvah, or a wedding. The songs themselves are sung in different Maqāmāt (modes), chosen specifically for the different occasions: (the Maqām is a general term for each of the modal systems upon which Middle-Eastern urban music (specifically Arab and Turkish) is based. The term Maqām includes both the notes of the scale within each mode and the rules which govern

---

[2]   Rabbi Yehuda Alharizi, *Tahkemoni*, Aliasaph Press, Warsaw, 1899. Chapter 18 and 24.

[3]   Amnon Shiloah, The Musical Tradition of the Iraqi Jews, in *Iraqi Jews Traditional Culture*, Institute for Research Iraqi Jewry, 1983. pp. 14–18.

[4]   ibid.

[5]   Rabbi Yehuda Alharizi, *Tahemoni* Chapter 46.

[6]   Rabbi David Lanedo, *The Tsadikim of Aleppo* (*Tsadikim* – wise or holy men), Dva'sh, Yosef Ben Matityahu 3, Jerusalem. 2nd edition 1980.

the hierarchy of the notes and their function within a given piece. Examples of these are: the opening note, passing notes, middle pauses and the closing note.

It is the custom, for instance, when celebrating the birth of a son, to have the leading melody performed in *Maqām Ṣabah*, or *Maqām Bayāt*. The whole service will accordingly be conducted in these modes. For the birth of a daughter *Maqām Bayāt* is used; for a *Bar–Mitzvah, Maqām Ṣabah*; for a bridegroom, *Maqām ʿAjam* is preferred. On these festive occasions the whole congregation joins in the singing, which is led by the cantor, and each occasion is identified with the special qualities of the *Maqām* used for it. This applies especially to the services of the Sabbath and on the *High Holy Days*.

Examples from the Sabbath service

In the Sabbath morning service there are various passages that are sung by the entire congregation. One such passage is *Nishmat Kol Ḥai* (All living Creatures), in the course of which certain parts are sung by the whole congregation, such as *ShavuʿotʿAniyyim El Adon, Kaddish* and others.

Within the span of one year the Pentateuch is read in its entirety, divided up into weekly portions. In the course of the year some Sabbaths have a special name usually connected with the weekly portion of the Tora associated with that Sabbath. Examples of these special Sabbaths are: The Sabbath of Song, the Sabbath of the Ten Commandments, the Sabbath of Vision, and so on.

The Sabbath of Song is so called because its weekly portion includes the Song of the Red Sea, which celebrates in wonderful poetic language the safe passage of the Children of Israel 'on dry land' through the parted waters of the Red Sea. The Song of the Red Sea is performed in many ways, each ethnic group having its own special style. In some congregations the worshippers chant standing, in rememberance of the trumpets blown by the priests (Cohaním), and accentuate the celebratory nature of the occasion. On these special Sabbaths it is customary to hire the services of the best cantors, in the hope that they will inspire the congregation in a worthy manner. (see Music Examples 1 and 2)

The height of spiritual involvement in the service is attained in most congregations on the *High Holy Days*, when the lively participation of the worshippers constitute a large choir, conducted by the cantor and always following his lead in the responsorial passages. Because the special prayers on the *High Holy Days* appear only once a year in the liturgical repertoire, the worshippers co-operate fully with the cantor, and often volunteer as soloists in certain of the passages. The solemnity of the atmosphere on these days of intense prayer heightens the pathos of the special hymns used: Hence the artistic beauty of the singing uplifts the worshippers and in the communal singing each member of the congregation feels closer to the divine spirit, helped by the special atmosphere created by the cantillation.

The Singing of the Baqqashot

Among the Sephardi communities it became an established custom, over the years, for the congregants to gather in the synagogue after midnight on the Sabbath eve,

THEN SANG MOSES

Then sang Moses and the children of Israel this song unto the LORD, and spake, saying, I will sing unto the LORD, for he hath triumphed gloriously: the horse and his rider hath he thrown into the sea.

The LORD is my strength and song, and he hath become my salvation: he is my God and I will prepare him an habitation: my father's God, and I will exalt him.

The LORD is a man of war: The LORD is his name.

Pharaoh's chariots and his host hath he cast into the sea: his chosen captains also are drowned in the Red Sea.

The depths have covered them: they sank into the bottom as a stone.

Y estonces cantó Moxé y hijos de Israel
A la cantiga la esta a Adonáy
Y dixeron por dezir
Cantaré a Adonáy que enaltecer se enalteció
Cavallo y su cuatreguador arronjo en la mar

Fuerte y salmeavle Yah y fue a mí por salvación
Este mi Dió y aformoziguárlohe
Dió de mi padre y enaltecérlohe

Adonáy barragán de pelea Adonáy su nombre

Cuatreguas de Par'ó y su fonçado arronjó en la mar
Y escogedura de sus capitanes fueron fundidos en mar Ruvio
Abizmos los cuvrieron
Descendieron en porfundinas como piedra

Music Example 1

THE CRY OF THE POOR

The first line under the music *Mama yo no . . . .* translates:

These verses are sung at weddings to the tune *Mama yo no quero*

You will hear the cry of the poor. You will listen to the lament of the impoverished and save them. And it is written: 'Sing joyfully, O righteous, before HASHEM; for the upright, praise is fitting'.

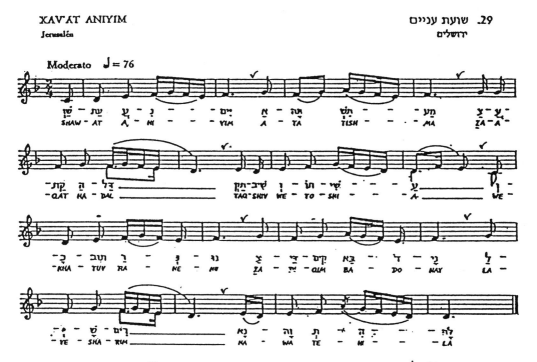

XAV'AT ANIYIM
Jerusalén

29. שועת עניים
ירושלים

Mama yo no quero

Esclamación de mesquinos tú oyes

Esclamación del prove escuchas y salvas

Y está escrito : Cantad justos con Adonáy

A los derecheros conviene loor

·(M.S.X.R.)

שׁוְעַת עֲנִיִּים אַתָּה תִּשְׁמַע
צַעֲקַת הַדַּל תַּקְשִׁיב וְתוֹשִׁיעַ
וְכָתוּב רַנְּנוּ צַדִּיקִים בַּאדֹנָי
לַיְשָׁרִים נָאוָה תְהִלָּה

Music Example 2

to perform hymns that were composed by various liturgical poets, often especially for that purpose. These hymns came to be known as *Baqqashot* (supplications).

On such winter nights the singers of the *Baqqashot* would form groups, and the groups vied with each other in an attempt to excel in their rendering of the hymns. This custom originated in the city of Safed, in Galilee, where members of the mystic Cabbalist sect ascribed special powers to prayers and hymns that were sung in the hours of the early morning watch.

The custom of the *Baqqashot* spread through the countries of the Mediterranean Basin, and volumes of hymns were compiled for them by the liturgical singers. The *Baqqashot* provided an inexhaustible source of material for cantors in the Oriental communities, who used them for complex improvisation in the different *Maqāmāt* (modes). The sessions of the *Baqqashot* were always attended by a large number of congregants, some active participants, but many as a passive audience. With the establishment of the *Baqqashot* in the synagogues, a new situation evolved. The synagogue could host musical events of a para-liturgical nature, that were not compulsory services (see Music Example 3).

Until the beginning of the 20th century, the Yoḥanan Ben-Zakai synagogue in Jerusalem hosted many musical happenings such as the singing of the *Baqqashot*. The style maintained was Sephardi, perpetuating to a large extent the melodies which the Jews of Spain (expelled in 1492 under the edict of the Inquisition), took with them into exile and guarded carefully. This style of singing disappeared when the Jews of Aleppo arrived in Jerusalem, the time when the Sephardi Jews first began to move beyond the confines of the Old Jewish Quarter of the Old City. The Aleppo style of *Baqqashot* filled the void left by the Sephardic families, and the tunes they introduced, mainly Oriental in nature, established an ascendancy in the liturgical repertoire, which still exists now, nearly one hundred years later. This tradition of concerts held by the cantors in the synagogue, unaccompanied by musical instrument soon caused a mingling of styles among the ethnic groups, and the pure Spanish tradition could no longer be maintained.

Other important musical events occur throughout the year. Between the Passover festival and Pentecost, The Song of Songs is sung festively each week[7] with the cantor and the congregation singing alternate verses. Nowadays, in the Sephardi synagogue a special effort is made to encourage the younger members of the congregation, who are required to step onto the central cantor's podium and sing the special hymns of praise as an informal choir. This practice is common in all the services. The children are expected to sing the cantor's verses of the Song of Songs with the congregation. The performance of the Song of Songs lengthens the service until sundown, the time for the traditional counting of the 'Omer.[8]

On the intermediate Sabbaths between Passover and Pentecost, the *Ethics of the Fathers* are sung. It is to be noted that there are six Sabbaths between Passover and Pentecost, which officially marks the giving of the law on Mt. Sinai, hence the traditional Pentecost reading of the Ten Commandments. The Tractate of the Fathers, (*Ma se het* 'Avot) is also read during this seven-week period. One of the six chapters is read on each of the interim Sabbaths between Passover and

---

[7]   In some communities the Song of Songs is performed throughout the year, not only between Passover and Pentecost.

[8]   The *'Omer* is counted every evening between Passover and Pentecost. It must be counted after sunset, and the Song of Songs is performed to use the interim time appropriately.

1

פיטן : חַי , חַי ;

קהל : אֵל מִסְתַּתֵּר בְּשַׁפְרִיר חֶבְיוֹן

הַשֵּׂכֶל הַנֶּעֱלָם מִכָּל רַעְיוֹן ;

עִלַּת הָעִילוֹת מוּכְתָּר בְּכֶתֶר עֶלְיוֹן

כֶּתֶר יִתְּנוּ לְךָ ה' .

חֲזַק מִיַחַד כְּאֶחָד עֶשֶׂר סְפִירוֹת

מַפְרִיד אַלוּף לֹא יִרְאֶה מְאוֹרוֹת ;

סַפִּיר גִּזְרָתָם יַחַד מְאִירוֹת

תִּקְרַב רִנָּתִי לְפָנֶיךָ ה' .

Music Example 3

Pentecost. The Ashkenazi congregations traditionally read the *Ethics of the Fathers* without singing until the Feast of the Tabernacles. The reciting of the tractate attracts many congregants to the synagogue, to hear the cantor's performance. A musical happening of this kind attracts people from all walks of life. The cantors exploit their material to the full chanting the passages in a way that is attractive to the congregation, while experimenting in the various *Maqāmāt*. They take a basic theme, and then veer away from it, undertaking daring improvisations within the appointed *Maqām*, and eventually returning to the melody after demonstrating their cantorial prowess. There is a process of change, whereby the younger listeners, unfamiliar with the original melody, imitate their favorite cantors, and thus the improvisation eventually becomes part of the theme.

In Summary

The new willingness to listen to the *Maqāmāt*, to which the Oriental ear is naturally tuned, accentuates the uplifting of the spirit and the aesthetic appreciation of the congregation, on all those occasions when singing is a means of achieving a deeper spiritual identification with the Divine.

Cantors, Composers and Educators in Our Time

The cantors and liturgical singers of the previous generation were, for the most part, outstanding and godfearing scholars (one of the necessary attributes of the cantor, according to Jewish Law, or *Halakhah*). The congregation related to them as such, for they served as mediators between the members of the community and the Creator.

In the nineteen-thirties Rabbi Ben-Tsion Meir Hai 'Uzziel, who was at that time the Chief Rabbi of Tel-Aviv,[9] asked the cantors Rabbi Nissim Korkidi and Nisan Cohen-Melamed[10] to establish a choir and a music seminary for Sephardi cantors. This was the first choir that was taught the prayer passages in a systematic way, just as the institute *Pirḥei–Kehunnah* was the first Sephardi cantors' seminary. Nisan Cohen-Melamed (1916–1993) himself composed 300 liturgical melodies, many of which were and still are very popular. He continued to direct the Sephardi cantors' seminary until the nineteen-sixties, apart from the years when he served as an emissary for Israel in Mexico and Iran.[11]

During this time other choirs were established in different parts of the country. In Jerusalem Raḥamim 'Ammar established choir that was affiliated to the *Zekhor Le'Avraham* synagogue.

Rahamim 'Ammar composed liturgical passages in various *Maqāmāt* and then in note form. (see Music Example 4)

---

[9]   From 1949–1963 Rabbi 'Uzziel served as the Chief Rabbi of Israel.

[10]   Rabbi Nissim Korkidi was the Cantor in the Ohel Mo'ed Synagogue, the most important Sephardi synagogue in Tel Aviv. Nisan Cohen-Melamed joined him there, first as reader from the Torah scroll, and later as Cantor in the synagogue services.

[11]   Akiva Tsimmerman, *Together in Song*, published by the central cantorial archive, Tel Aviv. 1987 (this archive is managed solely by A. Tsimmerman).

Nishmat Kol Hai

ALL LIVING CREATURES

Lord our God, the soul of all living creatures shall bless Thy name, the spirit of all flesh shall ever praise Thee and extol Thee, Our King.

From eternity to eternity Thou art God.

THE CRY OF THE POOR

You will hear the cry of the poor. You will listen to the lament of the impoverished and save them. And it is written: 'Sing joyfully, O righteous, before HASHEM; for the upright, praise is fitting' By the mouth of the upright shall You be exalted; by the lips of the righteous shall You be blessed; by the tongue of the devout shall You be sanctified; and amid the holy shall You be lauded.

Music Example 4

GOD OF THANKSGIVING

God of thanksgiving, Master of wonders, Creator of all souls, Master of all deeds, who chooses musical songs of praise – King, Unique One, God, Life-giver of the world.

Music Example 4 (Continued)

His choir used to appear on Israeli Radio on Friday afternoons in a special programme welcoming the Sabbath, that was produced by Ephraim Di-Zahav. For several decades this choir was one of the most popular in Israel, and was chosen to appear on many public festive occasions. Some of his pieces are preserved in the archives of the Institute of Jewish Music (Renanot), quite a few are performed regularly by choirs and singers, and are often still to be heard on the radio.

Distinguished Musicians

During this period, Ezra Aharon was becoming established as an 'oud player of great distinction. He took part in the congress on Arab Music that was held in Cairo in 1932. He also composed liturgical hymns that were performed by a choir that he formed in the nineteen-forties. He transcribed some of his melodies in note form. However, since he retired from his work as director of the Oriental music department of Israel Radio, his works have been performed less and less, except for one very famous melody set to the words of Rabbi Israel Najjara, *Ya'ala Ya'ala Bo'i Legani*, which is generally performed in the synagogue on the occasion of the birth of a daughter.

The late Asher Mizrahi, 1890–1967, was a Jerusalem born composer and cantor. During the years that he worked in Tunis he spread the Jerusalem cantorial tradition and the Sephardi style of prayer. In Tunis he established choirs that performed his melodies. Among his outstanding pupils are Rabbi Getz, the rabbi of the Western Wall, David Riyahi and Michael Sitbon. David Riyahi established a synagogue choir in Netanya that accompanied the services that he conducted, and which performed many of Asher Mizrahi's melodies. Asher Mizrahi was a prolific composer, and many of his melodies are to be heard, both within the framework of the synagogue and elsewhere, on festive public occasions.

The late Shaul 'Abbūd was an educator of great stature, who trained a whole generation of cantors and liturgical composers. He produced the book, *Hymns of Song*, effectively a guidebook for the *Baqqashot*, in accordance with the order of the *Maqāmāt*. He was one of the founders of the tradition of singing *Baqqashot* in Jerusalem. In the nineteen-thirties he established a choir whose members later served as cantors of repute, both in Israel and in other countries. Rabbi Israel Elnadaf, the late Moshe Ner-Ga'on, Aharon Ner-Ga'on, Rabbi Yosef Mutseri, and the late Rabbi David Shaharabani are but a few examples. In his book Shaul 'Abbud indicates the prescribed order of melodies for the Sabbath services and offers valuable advice for cantors who use the book, explaining which melodies to use within the structure of various *Maqāmāt*.

There were other choirs, set up in various synagogues, whose function was to enhance the synagogue services. Needless to say, none of these devoted cantors was remunerated for his work.

The late Yosef Almani (1908–1981) was born a tenth generation Israeli. He composed musical passages in different *Maqāmāt* that have become an integral part of the synagogue repertoire. He recorded his compositions on tape, but did not transcribe them. He was consistently faithful to the old Sephardi style, uninfluenced by prevalent Arabizing trends, except for his adherence to the framework of the *Maqāmāt*.

The late M. Ḥalfon (1926–1981) received his formal education from the late Raphael Mizrahi, the renowned teacher in the School for the Blind. He was taught the basis of the Turkish *Maqāmāt*, and the prayer cycle by Moshe Vital, one of the most well-known cantors of the previous generation, who introduced Ḥalfon to the World of Sephardi cantorial singing. Ḥalfon studied the *'oud*, Arabic music and composition with Ezra Aharon, according to the Egyptian school. In the nineteen-fifties Moshe Ḥalfon established the Ḥafetz Ḥaim choir, whose members were from the orphanage of the same name. Ḥalfon also composed liturgical music. His most famous melody is *Samaḥti Be'omrim Li Beit Hashem Nelekh* (Psalm 122) (see Music Example 5).

He was assisted in conducting the choir by Meir Levi, who now serves as cantor in the Damascus Ahiezer synagogue in New York.

The Institute of Jewish Music, *Renanot*, has initiated the composition of new liturgical music for the synagogue. The institute was founded in 1957, with these declared aims: to further knowledge of the musical traditions of the different ethnic groups; to collect, preserve, document and publish Jewish music; to further cantorship, both the reading of the Torah according to the accents and the singing of the synagogue services, with a view to improving their quality; the dissemination of Jewish music; the establishment of seminaries where cantors could learn their craft, each according to his specific ethnic tradition. The Institute of Jewish Music holds a congress of Jewish Music and a convention of cantors, annually, and concerts of cantorial music periodically. These events constitute a framework for researching the heritage of Jewish music over the generations, and for learning and teaching about Jewish musical composition in modern times.

Ḥaim Tsur is a composer and violinist, currently the director of the Folklore Department in the Israel Broadcasting Authority. The Institute for Jewish Music has commissioned many cantorial pieces from him, Including a set of hymns composed in *Maqām Nahawand*. He has also composed numerous songs, many of them for liturgical texts, which have become firmly established in the liturgical repertoire (see Music Example 6).

PSALM 122

I was glad when they said unto me Let us go into the house of the LORD.

Our feet shall stand within thy gates, O Jerusalem.

Jerusalem is builded as a city that is compact together:

Whither the tribes go up, the tribes of the LORD, unto the testimony of Israel, to give thanks unto the name of the LORD

For there are set thrones of judgement, the thrones of the house of David.

Pray for the peace of Jerusalem they shall prosper that love thee.

Peace be within thy walls, and prosperity within thy palaces.

For my brethren and companions' sakes, I will now say, Peace be within thee.

Because of the house of the LORD our God I will seek thy good.

Music Example 5

KEDUSHAH

During the repetition of the ʿ*Amidah*, the *Kedushah* is recited while standing.

Congregation with the Reader responding:

Let us revere and hallow Thee even as in the prophet's vision the choir of holy Seraphim hallowing Thy name in consecration "call to one another:

Congregation and Reader respond:

'Holy, holy, holy is the Lord of hosts,

His glory fills the whole earth.'

Congregation with the Reader responding:

Yea, the earth is filled with His glory. His ministering angels ask of one another, "Where is the abode of His glory?" Responding in blessing they say:

Congregation and Reader:

"Blessed be the glory of the Lord from His abode."

KEDUSHAH

Music Example 6

Rabbi Mordekhai Ashkenazi is one of the senior teachers in *Renanot*. He is both a cantor and a composer. The Institute has commissioned many liturgical compositions from him. The students of cantorship in *Renanot* learn his music and later perform it in synagogues where they conduct the services. Other cantors become familiar with his music from the radio and introduced it into their own repertoire.

The author, in his capacity as Director of *Renanot*, instituted courses in cantorship in 1984. The study programme includes: study of the prayer melodies in the different *Maqāmāt*; hymns associated with the specific *Maqāms* that are learned in the course; study of the *Baqqashot* as an integral part of the cantor's role; the biblical accents; voice development; illustrated lectures given by cantors, so that each graduate of the course will be culturally richer and fully equipped to undertake the duties of a cantor. When such a graduate takes up a post with a congregation, he does not create a new cantorial tradition, but makes use of what he has learned on the course. At time goes by, he will develop his talents to create his own original style. He may, in due course, compose new melodies which can then be included in other cantors' repertoires.

Cantorial Music in the Media

Until the nineteen-twenties the cantor's realm of influence was within the four walls of the synagogue, in the communal services or on the festive occasions when para-liturgical music was sung.

Radios, tapes, cassettes, television and video have changed that picture. The media provide a framework of reciprocal influence which enables liturgical music to be heard by a much wider audience, but which in turn has direct bearing on the popularity of the melodies. The relationship between the cantor, the congregation and the media is one of continuous reciprocal influence.

By the nineteen-twenties records of liturgical music performed by cantors were already available, and many people bought them Raḥamim 'Ammar's renderings were often played on the radio, thereby familiarizing the listeners with his music, which they in turn brought to the synagogues. This was a new channel, beyond the walls of the houses of prayer, for enriching the liturgical repertoire. It should be pointed out that until the nineteen-forties, most household in what was then Palestine did not have electricity. Only then were the majority of people able to purchase and enjoy their much-awaited radios.

Fresh waves of immigration after the establishment of the State of Israel in 1948 brought new and varying styles of liturgical music and cantorship into the country, reflecting the cultures of the many ethnic groups. The newcomers, like their predecessors received their share of radio exposure.

Within the Broadcasting Service Mr. Yosef Ben-Yisrael established a choir, *Shiru shir*, which held evenings of song, and also accompanied concerts of liturgical music, with the addition of an instrumental group. The performances of the choir, recorded by the radio and frequently broadcast, helped to popularize the liturgical music of the different ethnic groups.

With the establishment of Israel Television in the mid nineteen-sixties, a new phase of media interaction began. Programmes of liturgical music were broadcast at the special times allocated for religious documentary programmes. This was done for the *Selihot,* during the important weeks leading up to the Day of Atonement. Other genres of liturgical music were also transmitted, including the *Baqqashot* mentioned above. In the most natural way cantors absorbed new themes and concepts which gradually found their way into the synagogues. In the last twenty years an additional dimension has been added, the production of audio and video cassettes by cantors with expert knowledge of the *Maqāmāt.* In recent years *Renanot* has produced cassettes of whole services rendered in the styles of the different ethnic groups by expert cantors. This material is used by radio and television alike, and is marketed both in Israel and abroad.

Sources of Influence on the Melodies Used in the Synagogue

In the diaspora, the musical cultural environment always had a great impact on synagogue music, and there is no doubt that in modern times the influence has both increased and diversified. Most often heard in the synagogue are themes of popular secular Israeli songs, in addition to Greek and Turkish melodies. Israeli melodies that have been accepted in the synagogue include *Jerusalem of Gold, From the Summit of Mount Scopus, Evening of Roses* and many more. The melodies have been incorporated into various parts of the services, a process initiated by the cantor, but welcomed by the congregation, who know and love the tunes. There is no doubt that the style of the *muwashshaḥāt,* and in general the classical Arab style of singing, play an important part in the repertoire of the cantors, who hear this style of music on the regional Arab radio station. They have been even more exposed to the Arab musical style in recent years, as many of the songs have had popular Hebrew lyrics composed for them, and the cultural impact is tremendous.

In summary it can be said that singing in the modern Sephardi synagogue is a product of centuries of tradition. In recent decades cantorial music has moved beyond the intimate confines of the synagogue into public areas, including both the media of radio and television, and also the concert halls where liturgical concerts attract large audiences.

Translated by: Naomi Tsur

Musical Performance,
1997, Vol. 1, Part 2, pp. 81
Reprints available directly from the publisher
Photocopying permitted by license only

© 1997 OPA (Overseas Publishers Association)
Amsterdam B.V. Published in The Netherlands
by Harwood Academic Publishers
Printed in Singapore

A Guide to the Pronunciation of Words and Phrases

The transliteration of Arabic, Greek and Hebrew characters into Roman script is by its very nature imprecise. A number of characters in these languages have no direct equivalent in our script. Until comparatively recently no consistent transliteration has been observed and as a result many variants can be found in translated and original works in Western languages. We have sought to use the forms now generally considered to be the most accurate.

The following give an approximate indication of how the various accents may be interpreted and assist the reading of the texts.

ā   as in *calm*

'a   a strong guttural produced by the compression of the throat and expulsion of the breath

h   as in *h*at

ḥ   a strong aspirant as in *loch*

q   as *k* produced far back in the throat

ū   long, as in *clue*

'u   a strong guttural as in 'a above

′   within a word creates a break, similar to that after the first syllable in absolute, *or co'at* instead of *coat*

á   or í indicates an accented vowel

ĉ   as *ch* in *ch*ild

g   as in *go*

ĝ   as in the Italian Giovanni

ǰ, ĝi or ŝ as *j* in *j*eux in French

ñ as in o*n*ion

ś or će as *z* in *z*oo

š or ǰ as *sh* in *sh*e

All the song texts and words used in the article by Susana Weich-Shahak in part 2 are Judeo-Spanish, called *Judezmo* in the Balkans and *Hakita* in Morocco, and sometimes, mistakenly, called *Ladino*.

Musical Performance,
1997, Vol. 1, Part 2, pp. 83–86
Reprints available directly from the publisher
Photocopying permitted by license only

© 1997 OPA (Overseas Publishers Association)
Amsterdam B.V. Published in The Netherlands
by Harwood Academic Publishers
Printed in Singapore

A Glossary of Musical Terms

A

ahavah rabbah   a mode (steiger) corresponding to the phrygian mode
'ajam   name of a maqām
'atābā   an Arab folk song genre

B

baraban   a large cylindrical double skin drum played by Bulgarian Jews

C

Calqi   musician **calqici** (Turkish musicians)
Cancionero   anthology of songs called canticas, cantigas or canteres, strophic
      poems, often of four lines, with the second and fourth lines
      rhyming, with or without a refrain
cantadera   semi-professional female singer
cantares or **cantes**   songs (in Morocco)
canticas or **cantigas**   songs (eastern area)
cantigas de boda   wedding songs
cantigas de novia   wedding songs
cantigas de parida   songs for the circumcision
chalguí   musician **chalguiĝís** musicians (Turkish)
cimbal   dulcimer
compaña   company
copla(s)   strophic poems, composed mainly in the 18th century in Salonika,
      about Jewish values, beliefs, and views; their themes relate to the fes-
      tivities throughout the Jewish year, to historic events and happenings
      in the community, often with a didactic, moralizing intent.

D

darabukka
darbuga   } a goblet shaped drum
dumbelek
debkah   an Arab and Druze dance

E

El Adon   a Sabbatical and festival prayer hymn
endechas/oínas qinot   dirges
endechadera/oinaderas (pl.)   bewailer(s) those who sing endechas

G

ĝumbus   a fretted string instrument with a circular resonance cavity covered with skin. The strings are plucked with a plectrum.

H

hackbrett   dulcimer
ḥavurah   company
ḥavurot hazemer/ḥavurat renanim   song companies
Ḥazonis   (Yiddish) cantorial music
Ḥazzan   cantor (pl. Ḥazzanim)
Ḥazzanut   (i) a generic term for Ḥazzan (ii) cantorial/liturgical (improvised) music
ḥevrá   society
ḥevruta   company
ḥidā   an Arab folk song genre
hōra   an Israeli folk dance, a round dance

K

kadatcha   a popular dance at Hasidic weddings, it is mainly danced by men to fast klezmer music
kitka   (Bulgarian) a bouquet (of songs)
klezmer   musical instrument; also the name given to those itinerant musicians who travelled within the Jewish communities in central Europe

L

La esfuegra grande   the groom's mother

M

makam/makamlar   (Turkish)
maqām/maqāmāt   (Arabic) a generic word for mode
maqām bayāt   a mode that starts with a tetrachord of two 3/4 tones followed by a whole tone
maqām nahawand   name of a maqām with a minor scale
maqām rast   a mode that starts with a tetrachord of one whole tone followed by two 3/4 tones
mhorabe   Arab folksong genre
mijana   (or **mejana**) an Arab folk genre
mizmār   a double reed shawm (similar to an oboe)
muwashshaḥ/muwashshaḥāt   poetical strophic genre; also a vocal musical form
muwwal   vocal improvisation

N

nahawand   name of a maqām
nāy or **nai**   flute, open at both ends
niggun   (pl. **niggunim** tune or melody type)

nusaḥ prayer tune   (pl. **nusahim** [Hebrew]/**nusahot** [Aramaic] prayer tunes)

P

parida   mother of the new-born child
pandero } tambourine
panderico }
pandericos (pl) } tambourines
pandereta (pl) }
parmak zilí   finger cymbals played by women in the Turkish area
plañideras   mourners
preciadores   honourable men, trusted by the community, who evaluate the
    bride's dowry. This is then written into the wedding contract.

Q

qānūn   psaltery or zither – the strings of these instruments are plucked, in
    contrast to the dulcimer, cimbalom or cimbal on which they are struck.
qumbus   a fretted string instrument with a circular resonance cavity covered
    with skin. The strings are plucked with a plectrum.
qinot   dirges

R

renbetiko   a song sung by the Greek poor and disposed
Romancero   a collection of romance songs (settings of narrative poems) on me-
    dieval subjects – kings, queens and knights; palace intrigues,
    faithful and unfaithful wives; also biblical themes. The textual
    structure is a series of rhyming 16 syllable verses (divided into
    two hemistiches of 8). The musical structure, with one musical
    stanza recreated with slight variations.

S

sāgāt   small cymbal attached to the fingers
šarki   Turkish lyric songs; couplets or strophes about various unconnected sub-
    jects (usually love and longing)
sharqi   an Arab folk song genre
shofar   the traditional ramshorn sounded in the synagogue on High Holidays
    of the year
shubbaba   flute
silsul   ornate vocal passage
singerel   boy singer
sonaja   tambourine (western area)
steiger/steigerim   lit: scale/scales, meaning scale types (modes)
sullam   scale

T

tañedera   the pandero player who accompanies the cantadera
taqsīm   a form of instrumental improvisation in Arab music

tzimble   (Yiddish) cimbal

U

ʻūd or **oud**   short necked lute

Y

yarghūl or **urghūl**   an Arab single-reed instrument used to accompany folk
dances

Z

zemer   song
zimriyah   song festival.

Musical Performance,
1997, Vol. 1, Part 2, pp 87–90
Reprints available directly from the publisher
Photocopying permitted by license only

A Glossary of Other Words and Expressions

A

adar   the 5th month of the Hebrew calendar
'alakefak   a colloquial Arabic word meaning 'as you would like it'
'aliya   immigration to Israel
Alheña   a family feast enjoyed by Moroccan Sephardi Jews when, as a good omen, the bride's hands are painted with henna
Almosama   the feast in the bride's honour celebrated in Salonica by Jewish families
Ashkenazi (pl. Ashkenazim)   since medieval times refers to the Jewish area of settlement in north-west Europe; later, to the Jews of European and Russian background, with their distinctive liturgical practices and religious customs

B

ba'al-tefillah (pl. ba'ale-tefillah)   a cantor who is an expert in the performance of prayers
badhan   entertainer (jester/comedian), singer, master of ceremonies
baqqashot   supplications
bar mitzvah   a son arriving at confirmation*
bat mitzvah   a daughter arriving at confirmation*
          *[both refer to the occasion when a boy or girl reaches the age of religious majority and responsibility (a boy at 13; a girl at 12 years and a day)]
Belz   an Hasidic dynasty
Bnei 'Akiva   a religious youth movement
brit-mila   circumcision

C

C.E.   common or Christian era

D

dayyanim   judges
devekut   to pray (or sing or dance) with great devotion
diaspora   the dispersion of the Jews after the destruction of the Temple. Also used to describe the places to which they dispersed

E

Eretz-Yisrael   name used to designate Israel before the State of Israel had been established

G

galut   exile; the term used to refer to the various expulsions of Jews from their ancestral homeland, also 'homelessness' or the state of being in exile. To be in *galut* means to live in the diaspora

Gur   an Hasidic dynasty

GRC   General Record Company

H

Habad   an Hasidic dynasty

hafla   the Arabic term for a festive and social gathering

Hanukkah   festival of lights, celebrating the triumph of the Hasmoneans over the Greek army

haredi/haredim   Orthodox Jew(s), or ultra Orthodox Jew(s)

haskalah   the enlightenment

Hasid   a pious man. Follower of 18th century religious Hasidic movement

henna   a paste made from dried crushed leaves applied to parts of a bride's body at the henna ceremony

High Holy days   Rosh ha-shana (the Jewish New Year) and Yom Kippur (the day of atonement)

hillula   the joyous celebration of the sanctification of a revered public figure; a mass pilgrimage to the site of his burial

Histadrut   Israeli Federation of Trade Unions

HUC   Hebrew Union College (USA)

J

JTS   Jewish Theological Seminary (USA)

K

Kaddish   Consecration or Prayer for the soul of the dead

Ketav Rashi   a form of Hebrew writing or printing using special characters named after Rashi (the great commentator), used to write the commentaries of Biblical passages. It was also used to write Ladino and Judeo-Spanish until Ataturk's imposition of Latin characters for Turkish, as well as other influences that led the Sephardi Jews to change to Latin characters for writing Judeo-Spanish texts.

kibbutz/kibbutzim   the collective settlements in Israel

Kiddush   the benediction of the wine on Friday evening

L

ladino   the Judeo-Spanish in use among the decendants of the Jews expelled from Spain in 1792. Used only for the translation, word for word, of the Holy Scriptures, sacred books and prayers. Mostly another language, it is still in use, for instance, for the translation of the Pesah reading of the Haggadah and other festive liturgical texts

M

massekhet Avot   a Mishnah treatise
massoret   tradition
Mishnah   the collection of binding precepts which forms the basis of the Talmud and embodies the contents of the oral law of the Jews
mizraḥi (pl. mizraḥim)   Oriental, the name used to designate non-European Jews in general

O

'omer   (lit. 'sheaf'), an offering brought to the Temple on the second day of Passover; the name given to the period between Passover and Shavu'ot

P

peruch ha-milah   a real understanding of the word
Pesaḥ/Passover   the festival commemorating the Exodus from Egypt which marked the liberation of the Jews
pilpul   suble and skilful way of interpreting the Talmud that was frequently regarded as over-casuistic
piyyuṭ   religious poem
Purim   the festival commemorating the deliverance of the Jews, by Esther and Mordecai, from Haman's plot to kill them

R

Rashi   a great commentator of the scriptures (also see Ketav Rashi)
regalim   the three festivals of Passover, Shavu'ot, and Sukkot, during which a pilgrimage to the Temple must be accomplished
Rosh ha-shana   the Jewish New Year

S

sandaq   the person chosen to hold the male child at the ceremony of Circumcision
Shabbat   the Sabbath
seder   the order of the traditional service for Passover
sefat qodesh   Holy language
seliḥot   penitential prayers

Sephardi (pl. Sephardim)   since medieval times refers to those descended from the Spanish/Portugese Jews who lived in Spain before 1492; also those from the Balkans and the Middle East, in distiction to Ashkenazim, though it does not refer to all Jews who are not Ashkenazim

shaliyah tzibbur   a representative of the congregation

Shavu'ot   the festival of the first fruits which also celebrates the promulgation of the Torah (Pentecost)

sheva   a semi-vowel

shtetl   a small eastern European town largely inhabited by Jews

siddur   prayer book

simhat beit ha-sho'eva   ceremony of water-libation during the 7 days of Sukkot

steibels   small synagogues

Sukkot   the autumn harvest festival

T

Talmud   the record of the oral law compiled in Palestine and Babylonia in the 5th and 6th centuries

tefillah/tefillot   prayer/prayers

Torah   Jewish law. The Pentateuch

V

ve-af Hu   the beginning of a prayer

Viznitz   name of an Hasidic dynasty

Y

Ya'ala, ya'ala bo'i le-ganni'   the title of a song

Yad Vashem   the Holocaust Museum in Jerusalem, dedicated to the memory of those exterminated by the Nazis

yeshiva   Talmudic academy

Yiddish   an idiom combining Old German and Hebrew spoken by Ashkenazi Jews

Yishuv   'settlement' – the Jewish community in Palestine 1840–1948

YIVO   Institute for Jewish Research (New York)

Yom Kippur   day of Atonement

Z

zakhor   rememberance

Musical Performance,
1997, Vol. 1, Part 2, pp 91–92
Reprints available directly from the publisher
Photocopying permitted by license only

© 1997 OPA (Overseas Publishers Association)
Amsterdam B.V. Published in The Netherlands
by Harwood Academic Publishers
Printed in Singapore

Notes on Contributors

Ezra Barnea was born in Jerusalem in 1935. He is a graduate of the Hebrew University, in History and Jewish History, and the Teacher's Seminar. For 24 years a School Principal and then a Supervisor at the Ministry of Education from 1975, he also served as a Cantor for over 40 years. He was a Guest Lecturer at the Ben Gurion university from 1980 to 1982.

A Founder of the Central School of Cantors, Rananot, he is Director of the school and is in charge of producing recordings of every form of Jewish religious music of which,to date, they have made many versions.

Raymond Goldstein was born in 1953 in Capetown where he completed his musical studies. Since 1978 he has been a member of the vocal faculty of the Jerusalem Rubin Academy of Music. He also holds the post of music arranger/composer for the Jerusalem Great Synagogue Choir, where he has over 450 works to his credit. In 1991 he was appointed senior teacher at the Tel Aviv Cantorial Institute. As music director/accompanist, he frequently appears both on stage and on radio and television in Israel and has undertaken concert tours in Australia, USA and Western Europe. He has made professional recordings with international cantors and singers. His compositions include a chamber opera, works for chamber ensemble, and numerous arrangements, sacred and secular.

Jehoash Hirshberg, born in Tel Aviv, holds a Ph.D. in musicology from the University of Pennsylvania (1971). Now a professor at the Department of Musicology, Hebrew University, Jerusalem. Recent publications include Music in the Jewish Community of Palestine 1880–1948, A Social History, Oxford University Press. Other research fields: music of the fourteenth century in France, the music of the Karaite Jews, history of the early concerto.

Suheil Radwan was born in Nazareth in 1931. At the age of 20 he became the first music teacher in the Arab section. He was one of the first graduates of the Oranim Seminary where he had been a student in Abel Ehrich's class. His first degree in Arab and Islamic studies was gained at Haifa University and his Masters degree in Music Education at New York University. From 1966 until 1987 he was a music supervisor for the Arab section in the Ministry of Education and since 1990 has been the Director and conductor of the Arab Music Orchestra sponsored by the Rubin conservatory in Haifa.

Dr Natan Shahar was born in Israel and received his elementary high school education on a Kibbutz; he continued his studies at the Music Academy of the Hebrew University in Jerusalem. For many years he conducted choirs and instructed Song Groups. Over the past few years he has concentrated on musicological research. He has published articles and undertaken research on the Hebrew Song in its various socio-musical aspects. Natan Shahar is a lecturer at the Beit Berl College.

Amnon Shiloah was born in Argentina in 1928 and came to Eretz Israel in 1941 via Damascus. He earned his master's degree at the Hebrew University and a diploma at the Jerusalem Academy of Music (major subject: flute). In 1963 he was awarded a Ph.D. in musicology and Oriental studies from the Sorbonne in Paris.

He is now Morris and Dena Professor of Musicology at the Hebrew University of Jerusalem.

His specialized fields of research are in music of the Oriental Jewish communities and Arab music. He has played the flute with the Radio Symphony orchestra, and produced musical programs for Israel Radio.

In 1986 he received the Jerusalem prize for his scholarly works.

He has written extensively on near-eastern music history and on Arabic and Jewish music. Among his books: *The Theory of Music in Arabic Writings* (RISM, 1979); *Jewish Musical Traditions* (Wayne State University Press, 1992); *The Dimension of Music in Islamic and Jewish Culture* (Variorum, 1993); *Music in the World of Islam* (Scolar Press, 1995).

Musical Performance,
1997, Vol. 1, Part 2, pp. 93–95
Reprints available directly from the publisher
Photocopying permitted by license only

© 1997 OPA (Overseas Publishers Association)
Amsterdam B.V. Published in The Netherlands
by Harwood Academic Publishers
Printed in Singapore

Index

MUSICAL PERFORMANCE
AN INTERNATIONAL JOURNAL

Notes for contributors

Submission of a paper will be taken to imply that it represents original work not previously published, that it is not being considered for publication elsewhere and that, if accepted for publication, it will not be published elsewhere in the same form, in any language, without the consent of editor and publisher. It is a condition of acceptance by the editor of a typescript for publication that the publisher automatically acquires the copyright of the typescript throughout the world. It will also be assumed that the author has obtained all necessary permissions to include in the paper items such as quotations, musical examples, figures, tables etc. Permissions should be paid for prior to submission.

Typescripts. Papers should be submitted in triplicate to the Editors, *Musical Performance*, c/o Harwood Academic Publishers, at:

5th Floor, Reading Bridge House		820 Town Center Drive		3-14-9, Okubo
Reading Bridge Approach	or	Langhorne	or	Shinjuku-ku
Reading RG1 8PP		PA 19047		Tokyo 169
UK		USA		Japan

Papers should be typed or word processed with double spacing on one side of good quality ISO A4 (212 × 297 mm) paper with a 3 cm left-hand margin. Papers are accepted only in English.

Abstracts and Keywords. Each paper requires an abstract of 100–150 words summarizing the significant coverage and findings, presented on a separate sheet of paper. Abstracts should be followed by up top six key words or phrases which, between them, should indicate the subject matter of the paper. These will be used for indexing and data retrieval purposes.

Figures. All figures (Photographs, schema, charts, diagrams and graphs) should be numbered with consecutive arabic numerals, have descriptive captions and be mentioned in the text. Figures should be kept separate from the text but an appropriate position for each should be indicated in the margin of the typescript. It is the author's responsibility to obtain permission for any reproduction from other sources.

Preparation: Line drawings must be of a high enough standard for direct reproduction; photocopies are not acceptable. They should be prepared in black (india) ink on white art paper, card or tracing paper, with all the lettering and symbols included. Computer-generated graphics of a similar high quality are also acceptable, as are good sharp photoprints ("glossies"). Computer print-outs must be completely legible. Photographs intended for halftone reproduction must be good glossy original prints of maximum contrast. Redrawing or retouching of unusable figures will be charged to authors.

Size: Figures should be planned so that they reduce to 12 cm column width. The preferred width of line drawings is 24 cm, with capital lettering 4 mm high, for reduction by one-half. Photographs for halftone reproduction should be approximately twice the desired finished size.

Captions: A list of figure captions, with the relevant fegure numbers, should be typed on a separate sheet of paper and included with the typescript.

Musical examples: Musical examples should be designated as "Figure 1" etc., and the recommendations above for preparation and sizing should be followed. Examples must be well prepared and of a high standard for reproduction, as they will not be redrawn or retouched by the printer.

In the case of large scores, musical examples will have to be reduced in size and so some clarity will be lost. This should be borne in mind especially with orchestral scores.

Notes are indicated by superior arabic numerals without parentheses. The text of the notes should be collected at the end of the paper.

References are indicated in the text by the name and date system either "Recent work (Smith & Jones, 1987, Robinson, 1985, 1987) ..." or "Recently Smith & Jones (1987) ..." If a publication has more than three authors, list all names on the first occurrence; on subsequent occurrences use the first author's name plus "et al." Use an ampersand rather than "and" between the last two authors. If there is more than one publication by the same author(s) in the same year, distinguish by adding a,b, c etc. to both the text citation and the list of references (e.g. "Smith, 1986a") References should be collected and typed in alphabetical order after the Notes and Acknowledgements sections (if these exist).
Examples:
Benedetti, J. (1988) *Stanislavski*, London: Methuen
Granville-Barker, H. (1934) Shaekspeare's dramatic art. In *A Companion to Shakespeare Studies*, edited
        by H. Granville-Barker and G.B. Harrison, p. 84. Cambridge University Press
Johnson, D. (1970) Policy in theatre. *Hibernia*, **16**, 16.

Proofs. Authors will receive page proofs (including figures) by air mail for correction and these must be returned as instructed within 48 hours of receipt. Please ensure that a full postal address is given on the first page of the typescript so that proofs are not delayed in the post. Authors' alterations, other than those of a typographical nature, in excess of 10% of the original composition cost, will be charged to authors.

Page Charges. There are no page charges to individuals or institutions.